Confronting the Future:
A Conceptual Framework
for Secondary School
Career Guidance

Confronting the Future: A Conceptual Framework for Secondary School Career Guidance

THOMAS L. HILTON
Senior Research Psychologist
Educational Testing Service

In collaboration with

Gary J. Echternacht
Research Scientist
Educational Testing Service

Bruce L. Taylor
Director of Developmental Planning Analysis Administration
Educational Testing Service

Edward R. Tibby
Associate Director
College Board Western Regional Office

Raymond G. Wasdyke
Director of Programs for Vocational Education
Educational Testing Service

COLLEGE ENTRANCE EXAMINATION BOARD
New York • 1979

Copies of this book may be ordered from College Board
Publication Orders, Box 2815, Princeton, New Jersey 08541.
The price is $9.50.

Editorial inquiries concerning this book should be directed to
Editorial Office, College Entrance Examination Board,
888 Seventh Avenue, New York, New York 10019.

Library of Congress Catalog Card Number: 78-74228.

Printed in the United States of America.

Contents

Preface

The initial version of this volume was prepared as a conceptual framework for a long-range developmental program at Educational Testing Service and the College Board in the area of secondary school career guidance. At an early stage of the effort, the decision was made to share with a broader audience those parts of the design work that might be of general interest. This book is the result of that decision.

The team responsible for the design work was made up of the authors and six other ETS and College Board staff members who served as participants in our many discussions, as sources of ideas and advice, and as reviewers and critics — sometimes severe. These six were T. Anne Cleary and Linda A. Pfister of the College Board, and Martin R. Katz, Arthur M. Kroll, Ivor J. Thomas, and Wesley W. Walton, all of ETS. Although the contributions of these six members were invaluable, the authors assume full responsibility for what is written herein.

In its work the design team received the full cooperation of the officers of ETS and the College Board and, as far as we know, general support for the positions taken by the team. (We say "general support," for there no doubt is disagreement with many particulars.) Nevertheless, the positions espoused in this book should in no way be regarded as the official position of ETS or the College Board.

What the book does represent is the majority view of a group of ETS and College Board staff members who spent varying fractions of their time for approximately a year asking themselves what they would do if, starting from scratch, they were to design an ideal career guidance system for a secondary school. As will be seen, many wheels were reinvented, and we shamelessly borrowed ideas from our colleagues and the pioneers in career guidance, usually without acknowledging sources. We hope, however, that the wheels are put together in a way that represents a contribution and that our efforts will advance career guidance in this country.

Of the many ETS staff members who helped in the preparation of the manuscript, two deserve special recognition: Miriam Godshalk, and Frances Livingston. We also wish to express our indebtedness to the presidents of ETS and the College Board. William Turnbull and Sidney P. Marland, Jr., the providers of our daily bread — for which we give thanks — have been more than that; each provided intellectual stimulation, personal guidance, and generous support.

Thomas L. Hilton
Educational Testing Service

Introduction

Since the early sixties in this country there has been a growing concern that we have created a social environment that has seriously reduced the opportunities of our youth and the ease with which they move into the adult world (see Borow, 1966). Recently the National Panel on High Schools and Adolescent Education and Welfare, commissioned by the Department of Health, Education, and Welfare, noted that our society has, in the pursuit of universal education, "decoupled the generations" and that "we have succeeded in producing a youth society housed in an overburdened institution excessively isolated from the reality of the community and adult world (National Panel, 1974).

The Task Force on Secondary Schools in a Changing Society of the National Association of Secondary School Principals makes this strikingly parallel observation in its report entitled *This We Believe:*

> Physically, today's youth mature early. They exhibit an intellectual precocity and social awareness unmatched by previous generations. Yet, they are set aside by society. Most are asked to assume only minor responsibilities. Although fully ready to contribute to the world's work they are instructed to wait longer than did their parents or grandparents for that day of contribution. . . . Society loses their talents and they, in turn, lose the opportunity to mature through the assumption of responsible roles (NASSP, 1975, p. 16).

Contemporary secondary schools and their programs, as currently constituted, do not hold great promise for dealing with this societal malaise. The NASSP report further states:

> The routes available to youth to become adults are insufficient. The artificiality of the present arrangement must be amended by the adoption of authentic experiences. The adult world should be recoupled with youth . . . and youth should have learning opportunities in the practical and specific realm as well as those which are vicarious and theoretical (NASSP, 1975, p. 16).

The evolving idea of "career education" as described by Sidney Marland (1970) and others appears to hold promise for dealing with these problems. The implementation of this global idea will, however, require the development of new concepts in the areas of secondary school instruction and guidance functions. This book is devoted to a conceptualization of a comprehensive career guidance system for secondary school students. In presenting this conceptualization, we have tried to discuss all the elements and implications of such a system and to include the practical issues of what is needed to develop an operational system based on these concepts. In addition, we have suggested a framework for the research and development activities that will be required to implement the conceptualized system.

To keep the book within manageable limits, our focus is on career guidance functions at the secondary school level. We recognize, however, that preparation for careers must begin at the elementary school level. Any guidance systems at the secondary school level must be articulated with efforts at levels both below and above it to move students from awareness of the need for planning careers into the exploration of careers and thence to the specification of careers.

Our objective is to develop a truly comprehensive guidance system in several senses. First, it should serve the needs of all secondary school students whether they plan to continue their education, to seek employment after graduation, or to interrupt their education before graduation. Second, the system should be comprehensive with respect to functions, orientation, assessment, instruction, planning of work-related experiences, counseling, placement, evaluation, and follow-up. Third, the system should be comprehensive in terms of all educational levels — from the individual student, to the school, to state agencies. Thus, the needs of the student, the needs of the local school, the needs of the local school district (or other units intermediate between the schools and the state government), and the needs of state agencies must be considered.

Finally, our objective is comprehensive as far as the many aspects of student development are concerned. Intellectual development, personality development (especially self-knowledge and awareness), and the development of occupational knowledge and awareness are all critical aspects of career development and must be basic objectives in a comprehensive plan.

There are, however, two respects in which our system is not comprehensive. First, it focuses on career guidance. Although the learning problems, the personal problems, and the interpersonal problems of students are important aspects of the work of most high school guidance counselors, we will not discuss them here except as they relate to career guidance. Our concern is with career counseling as one aspect of guidance counseling. This is not to say that career counseling can in practice be divorced from guidance counseling. A socioemotional problem can prevent a student from gaining self-awareness. A learning disability can prevent a student from gaining a knowledge of occupations. But in one book we cannot do justice to all aspects of counseling and will not try.

Second, we do not explicitly discuss the crucial role of the family and of the community in student career development. The school system we discuss is embedded in this larger social context, but the complex and important interdependencies among the elements of this larger context — schools, parents, community service organizations, government agencies, employers, labor organizations, school boards, and taxpayers — need broader consideration than the scope of the present book will permit.

Whether we are talking about career education is an intriguing question. Our impression is that the only difference between career guidance (as we will discuss it) and career education (as it is discussed in the current literature) is that we will not discuss the content of the high school curriculum per se. It is not necessary, however, to grapple with the question here. We agree with Sidney Marland's well-known position that current efforts to correct the illnesses of our schools should not be constrained by precisely defined labels. The need is for imaginative and vigorous innovation and action, not quibbling over semantics.

We are not unmindful, however, of the likely long-range implications of the comprehensive system we propose. Attention to the cumulative impact of innovations is of critical importance, and we propose in Chapter 6 some steps that might be taken along these lines.

Although agreement on the definition of career education is not essential to our position, agreement about the need for innovation is. What, then, are the illnesses mentioned above? We would describe them as follows:

1. Too many students find high school a period of meaningless imprisonment.
2. Too many students flounder from one course to another, or from one school to another, without a goal or without the skills and insight to select a goal.
3. Too many of the high school population either leave school prior to graduation or graduate without the skills to obtain and sustain employment and without the motivation to continue their learning.

Our purpose is to conceptualize a guidance system that is responsive to these problems and that will at the same time serve as a framework for research and developmental activities throughout the country. We are by no means proposing a single program that all schools or students should pursue. The initial discussion is largely theoretical, focusing on an ideal that may take years to implement. Later sections deal with the realities of implementing a comprehensive system and include a number of steps that can be taken in the near future, many of which have already been taken by one or more schools in the United States.

We cannot possibly acknowledge all the many school systems, experimental projects, books, and articles that have stimulated our thinking and have suggested many of the ideas set forth in this book. Career guidance has a long history. Few ideas in contemporary guidance theory and practice are original, and the following are not necessarily exceptions. If the conceptualization has any originality, it lies in the way we have integrated, into one system, various components that are now in place in one school or another somewhere in the United States.

CHAPTER 1

Some Basic Assumptions about Career Guidance

Underlying our perception of the components of a comprehensive career guidance system are a number of assumptions about the goals of career guidance at the secondary school level, the nature of American high schools, and the nature of career development and decision making. These assumptions must be made explicit at the outset of our discussion of a comprehensive guidance system.

Assumption 1. When students leave high school, either before or at graduation, they should have carefully planned the next step of their careers and should take this step with as much knowledge as is possible of its probable implications for their developing careers.

This first assumption concerns a key objective of any career guidance program. But this objective does not imply that students should have fully developed plans for the rest of their lives. Not only is this unrealistic in terms of the self-insight and occupational awareness that most students are likely to have at the time they leave high school, but also it assumes a kind of stability and predictability in our cultural and occupational environment that is unwarranted, as expressed in our second assumption.

Assumption 2. In our rapidly changing world, individuals must have the ability and motivation to adapt to changing environmental demands and opportunities and to keep their options open. Career plans properly are perennially tentative, constantly subject to change.

We live in a culture that is in a rapid state of flux. Formal education, as we have known it, is changing, becoming more flexible and extended in time. The rigid pattern of 12 or 16 years of continuous lockstep school attendance is no longer the rule. Self-initiated interruptions in high school or posthigh school education are commonplace. Opportunities for adult education are burgeoning.

This growing adaptability of our educational structures is an inevitable result of developments in science and technology, of fundamental changes in our cultural traditions, mores, and institutions, and of the growing economic interdependence of nations. New means of transportation and communication, new sources of energy, new conditions of work, recreation, and religious observance, new components of responsible citizenship, new roles for men and women, new roles for members of the family, and increasing amounts of leisure time — all place unprecedented pressures on education in our society, pressures to create an educational environment in which our young people will develop into the kind of individuals demanded by their times.

We really cannot say what kind of individuals will be demanded by the next decade. Among futurists there is little consensus about anything except that there will be change. The priority needs of the job market 10 years from now are certain to be different from those of the present. To us this can only mean that there will be a premium on individuals, both young and old, who have the skills and, probably more important, the mental set to handle the stress of uncertainties and to make changes in their occupations, their personal goals, and their social and community affiliations.

Assumption 3. The career guidance needs of individual students vary over a broad spectrum; what is suitable for one student may well be a needless burden to another.

The multiplicity of possible student goals and student needs places a premium in guidance services on breadth, versatility, and recognition of the individuality of each student. Each student *is* different. Previews of vocational programs will appeal to some but not all students, in the same way that college interviews, plant visits, course selection training, and other services will have differential appeal. The traditional goal of some high schools to maximize college attendance is becoming an antiquated notion that can only result in misallocation of guidance resources. Similarly, to judge a vocational-technical department or school solely by the number of graduates it places immediately in jobs is an imperfect, although important, criterion. Surely the student who, through vocational instruction, discovers the value of advanced knowledge and enrolls in a university after graduation should be counted as a success of the department or school.

Assumption 4.   It is important for students to gain an understanding of what it means to earn a living and what this requires.

Although holding a job is probably the best way of acquiring such understanding, we would not recommend this as a required part of the high school experience for all students because of the differences in individual student needs. Nevertheless, encouraging students to gain knowledge of work and helping them toward that knowledge are, in the system we propose, significant career guidance functions.

Assumption 5.   Academic instruction and work-related experiences gain meaningfulness to students and increased valence when students understand the possible relevance of these experiences to their future work and to productive use of leisure time.

To make school and community experiences meaningful to the students in terms of their future life work is a function shared by the teaching and guidance staffs. This is not to say that academic instruction gains meaningfulness *only* through career relevance. Skillful teaching can make most content intrinsically interesting, but career relevance can contribute importantly to making course content meaningful, and thus it can increase the students' motivation to master the content. Such meaningfulness implies a number of conditions: that students be oriented to the future, that instruction and work-related experience, in fact, have career-relevant elements, and that the school staff be cognizant of the relevance. To achieve that relevance, many high schools are currently engaged in extensive in-service training. In an informal telephone survey of guidance directors conducted by the authors, such training emerged as a high priority need.

Assumption 6.   Career development is a continuous interactive process, inextricably meshed with the total development of the student as a person.

For at least the last 20 years of theory development in career psychology, it has been recognized that career development, like cognitive development, is a process that cannot take place independently of other aspects of personal development. A career decision can be viewed as a joint function of the individual's personality, the momentary state of the environment, and past career decisions made by the individual. Everything we know (or hypothesize) about personality development, then, is relevant to career development. A number of career psychologists have proposed—and, to some extent, documented—stages in career development (Ginzberg, 1951; Super, 1953; and Crites, 1969). Although we lack any hard evidence to support the position, we can speculate that continuing research in the areas of career development and personality development will reveal structures and developmental processes that are common to each. Stages of career development may, for example, proceed in conjunction with Piaget's stages of cognitive development.

This is speculation, however. We discuss the subject here in support of the position that efforts to facilitate career development cannot be considered without regard for other aspects of the student's development. The instructional staff and the guidance staff are, indeed, in partnership, along with every other school, family, and community influence that has an impact on student development.

Assumption 7. Decision making relevant to careers continues throughout high school, and in later life as well, and certain early decisions frequently have a critical bearing on subsequent options open to the student.

This assumption follows from the previous one and also from the concept that a student's career opportunities and plans typically represent the accretion of a long chain of choices. At any point in time a student is likely to be on an educational pathway that to some extent limits his or her options at the next decision point. This is the natural consequence of the curriculum structure of most high schools and the sequential nature of most academic and vocational subjects. Unless a high school junior has taken an introductory language course, for example, he or she ordinarily cannot take an advanced language course.

In some high schools—hopefully declining in number—the

curriculum structure is such that certain early decisions seriously constrain the options open to the students later. In one high school studied intensively by the staff of ETS's Growth Study (Hilton, Beaton, and Bowers, 1971) the choice of ninth-grade mathematics was an extreme example of such a decision. Of the students who enrolled in algebra I, 95 percent subsequently graduated from the college preparatory program, and 75 percent of these graduates planned to go on to higher education. Of those who chose business arithmetic, none graduated from the college preparatory program, although 30 percent did plan to continue their education. Such statistics could represent the outcome of a benign and perfectly functioning sorting system, but we seriously doubt it. We would hope that this particular high school is not typical of many United States high schools, but we are confident in asserting that all high high school students are confronted with similar decisions—at different times and in respect to different educational pathways. How critical the choices are at each decision point will depend on the structure of the curriculum in each high school and the ease with which students can transfer from one pathway to another.

Assumption 8.   The first ingredient of successful career decision making is valid self-knowledge, and this self-knowledge is best obtained through self-analysis of relevant personal experiences.

All theoretical models of individual career decision making require the individuals to have a reasonably accurate image of themselves—their unique strengths, their interests and preferences, and, especially, their values (Katz, 1963). Accordingly, the quality of student decision making will depend directly on the accuracy of their self-perception. If their self-perceptions are seriously askew, their decisions will be equally so. And a bad decision may be worse than none at all.

Thus, the acquisition of valid self-insight is a crucial aspect of career development, perhaps the most crucial. How one best gains such insight is a central question that, to the best of our knowledge, remains unanswered. We are assuming, for our present purposes, that self-analysis of relevant personal experiences is likely to be most effective, although we know of no hard evidence in support of this position.

The traditional school, by means of conventional grades, provides the students with some indication of how their cognitive skills compare to those of their classmates. The relevance of such labeling to career planning is questionable, however. How much does a grade of B in history tell a student about his or her likely satisfactions in pursuing a given career (even though the grade may forecast quite accurately how well he or she will do in future history courses)? Would it not be more helpful for students to receive an evaluation of their performance that tells them something about their unique strengths and weaknesses, for example, their ability to understand complex causal influences?

As for interests and preferences, most guidance offices make standardized tests available to students. These, typically, inform the student of the similarity of his responses to those of adults in selected occupations. The shortcomings of these instruments have been widely discussed in the research literature. The question is whether students have sufficient bases to judge accurately their preference for one value or activity over another. Can adolescents say with sufficient certainty that it is more important to them to be of service to others than to earn a high income? Or that they would rather work outdoors than in an office? What real basis has the typical student for such judgments?

Not only have the students had limited work experience, but chances are that they have limited opportunity to glean from the experience any insight into their personal characteristics, particularly their developing values. Insight is not necessarily an automatic outcome of personal experience. Rather, it comes from thoughtful, deliberate planning and selection of academic and work-related experience and from equally thoughtful analysis of the outcomes — the successes and failures, satisfactions and frustrations, the heightened interests and the disillusionments. Furthermore, the sensitivity and analytical skill to learn from experience are not traits with which all young people are endowed, although our working hypothesis is that everyone has the capacity to develop them. The high school period is a time for acquiring these skills, and facilitating the acquisition of the skills is a key function of career guidance.

Assumption 9. The second ingredient of successful career decision making is an accurate knowledge of those occupations that are relevant to each individual student.

This knowledge includes cognitive, psychosocial, and physical demands (for example, skills, experience, education), the formal entry requirements (such as academic credentials, union member-ship), the time demands and working conditions, the current and future availability of jobs, the typical levels of compensation, likely gratifications of needs and values, opportunities for career advance-ment, if any, and possible barriers to advancement, if any. Also needed is information about state employment agencies, and about how labor unions function, especially in obtaining training, em-ployment, and job security. Perhaps most important, young people need a knowledge of economics, of the relation between employment and production, between supply of labor and demand, between in-flation and real income. Otherwise the schools may be guilty of the kind of deception with which Grubb and Lazerson (1975) have charged the proponents of career education, that is, of misleading students into believing there are no limits to career advancement, providing the individual is prepared and diligent.

Thus, successful decision making requires both a knowledge of self and a knowledge of occupations—and of how the two interact. Expecting all students to gain an accurate knowledge of all occupa-tions is both unrealistic and unnecessary. This position does, how-ever, introduce the problem of identifying the subset of occupations which are relevant to an individual student—a compelling reason for early occupational exploration.

Assumption 10. The primary motivation for student educational devel-opment derives from attainment by the student of high standards of excellence.

Whether in the classroom, the laboratory, or the shop, the stu-dent's motivation to pursue further a particular subject or skill is based primarily on a sense of personal accomplishment from his or her first exposure to it. This sense of accomplishment—which can range from the attainment of understanding, to the achievement of artistry or craftsmanship, to the correction of an equipment mal-function—places a premium on teachers who are informed in what constitutes excellence in a particular academic or vocational pur-suit, in what is within the reach of an individual student, and in how she or he can help the student achieve a sense of worthy performance.

These remarks are offered as an expression of our deep concern that no step recommended in the following chapters will in any way lower the caliber of school instruction, the professional standards of the teaching staff, or the quality of the curriculum. Although we repeatedly argue for career relevance in the curriculum, this relevance must never be achieved at the cost of excellence in instruction or reduction in the breadth and richness of the school program. As expressed in Assumption 5, relating course content to future work and productive use of leisure time lends meaningfulness to the school experience. But no amount of career relevance can justify a course that is dull, ineptly taught, empty of substance, and lacking in standards of excellence.

In concluding our listing of the assumptions underlying the proposed career guidance system, we remind the reader that these are, indeed, assumptions. Although we regard them as highly plausible, we recognize that alternative positions can be taken, and we would be hard put to refute them. Consider Assumption 10, for example. Is the attainment of excellence really the primary source of motivation? B. F. Skinner (1953) would probably agree. But others (see Strong, 1943, for example) would argue that motivation derives primarily from interests. Which position is more defensible is a matter of empirical research, as is the case in question after question which we raise in this book. If we achieve nothing more than to convince the reader of the pressing need for accelerated research on student learning and development, we will be satisfied. Meanwhile, back in the schools, the best we can do is make some educated guesses (assumptions) about what is primary and necessary and proceed from there.

CHAPTER 2

The Components of a
Student Guidance System

Implementing the kind of early planning, exploration, evaluation, and self-analysis implied by the 10 assumptions outlined in the previous chapter imposes an elaborate set of requirements on the school. These are presented in this chapter in roughly chronological order as 15 components of a comprehensive career guidance program. Although we are not unmindful of financial and practical considerations, the question of feasibility will be postponed until later chapters.

Component 1. Assessment, at or before high school entrance, of the student's personal characteristics and the status of his or her career planning.

The purpose of such assessment is primarily to initiate planning activity. The student who has not thought about his or her future and has no strategy for developing future plans needs to be confronted with the necessity for planning and exploration as early as possible in his or her high school career.

The concept of early confrontation is central to this book. It is our conviction that the primary need in high school career guidance is not for guidance materials — most school guidance libraries are adequately stocked with occupational literature (although quality and accessibility vary widely). The primary need is for a set of school procedures to start students thinking about self-assessment and career exploration early in high school. How best to achieve this is an unsolved problem that should receive priority of consideration. If nothing else, the students should be questioned about their career development strategies and should be required tentatively to evaluate the adequacy of these strategies.

Such assessments should not only stimulate actions by the students and provide them with relevant diagnostic information, but they should also provide information for teachers, counselors, and administrators at various levels to use in making informed educational management decisions in the interests of advancing student development.

We realize that such assessment, as well as steps we recommend later, could seriously strain the guidance facilities of most high schools. However, we are focusing here on an ideal model. Later we discuss the pressing practical problem of delivering the required services, recognizing that compromises may be necessary.

Component 2. Student selection of high school courses on the basis of their relevance to the student's developing plans or strategy for developing plans.

Such selection requires, most of all, information about where a particular course is likely to lead and the significance that successful or unsuccessful performance in the course may have. Each course taken should be regarded as a sample of the learning activities required by various classes of careers. The student needs answers to questions such as the following:

Generally what is the nature of the educational experience in the particular course? What is the purpose of the instruction? What subject matter is covered? What knowledge and skills should be acquired as a result of the course? By what means is evaluation of progress made? By the student? By others?

What attributes are needed for successful performance in the course? What initial knowledge and skills? What preferences, interests, and learning styles will contribute to successful performance?

Is the subject matter of the course especially relevant to any particular careers?

What personal needs are likely to be satisfied by the course, and what new, expanded needs are likely to be acquired by the student?

What unique attributes does the student have vis-à-vis the attributes required for the course?

Where is the instruction in a particular course likely to lead? What courses are likely to come next? And, in following years? If the course in question is selected, what opportunities is the student likely to have to change his or her educational program later in high school? How difficult will it be to switch later to another sequence of courses? What options typically have been open on graduation to students who have followed the sequence of courses that begin with the course in question?

Finally, and probably most important, to what extent are these options compatible with the particular student's posthigh school plans, however tentative they may be?

If, early in high school, the student has no definite posthigh school plans (which is likely to be the case for most students — and properly so), it is critical that options be kept open. Students should not commit themselves early in high school to a particular educational pathway without extensive self-assessment, occupational awareness and exploration, and career planning. But the sooner students engage in informed and skillful consideration of careers, the more profitable should be the secondary school experience. Course selection represents an opportunity to explore a range of academic and vocational instruction. Taking a course in auto mechanics can be an opportunity for a student to test his or her perception of auto repair as an occupation, or to get some feeling for related fields, such as mechanical engineering, or to acquire some skills which may enhance the future use of leisure time.

To consider the use of leisure time in a discussion of career guidance implicitly extends the definition of the term *career* to encompass all future time expenditures of the individual, including those for which no monetary compensation is received. In other words, *career* becomes synonymous with *future,* and instead of referring to *career* awareness, we could just as well refer to *future* awareness. Career education could become *future-oriented* education or *life* education. But this is not helpful, for such a definition becomes so all-encompassing that it provides little basis for decision making. We wish there were some way out of this semantic swamp, but as yet we have not discovered it. We can only say we do not believe that every secondary school course should have direct or immediate vocational relevance. Some may be more relevant to the enrichment of leisure time or the sheer and simple enjoyment of life. Teenagers are not adults, and the teen years present a chance for wide-ranging, adventurous exploration. Nevertheless, when a student elects a course for the sheer fun of it, the decision to do so should be a deliberate, informed decision and he or she should regard the experience as an opportunity to gain self-knowledge.

Component 3. At the completion of each academic or vocational course, review by students of the possible career implications of their experience in the course.

What meaning does the student's performance have as far as her or his tentative plans are concerned? If the student experienced difficulty in the course or found the learning activity dissatisfying, what conclusions might be drawn? Did successful performance, in retrospect, require skills that the student did not possess? Or did successful performance require a learning style that was not compatible with the unique preferences of the student? Did the student find it difficult to summon the motivation for successful performance in the course? If so, why?

Generalizing from a single course is, at best, risky. Teachers are not uniformly successful in stimulating the interests and best efforts of all students. Any observer of the academic process can cite cases of students who have rejected a whole cluster of careers on the basis of a single unfortunate academic or vocational experience. Occupations requiring complex numerical skills seem to be frequent examples. We wonder how many young people have rejected careers in science and engineering on the basis of a single defeating experience in a high school mathematics course. Or how many students have given up the idea of a career in medicine or nursing simply because of an unstimulating and unrewarding chemistry course. In general, the authors' observation is that the experience a student has in a particular high school course plays a more significant role in forming occupational preferences than is generally recognized.

The more important function of career guidance at this level may therefore be to reduce the tendency of students to overgeneralize from small samples of learning activity that they perceive, frequently erroneously, as typical of the cognitive or psychomotor activity required by a particular occupation. Nevertheless, even in the best schools, students have limited opportunity to sample the content of occupations, and those opportunities that are present must be milked of their meaning. The cumulative impact of classroom, laboratory, and shop experiences should have meaning that single experiences lack.

Component 4.   Valid occupational sampling by the student.

This is essential to the development of career plans and constitutes a critical ingredient in a comprehensive guidance system. The need is widely recognized. Most high schools now provide the student with opportunities for occupational exploration through classroom, shop, and laboratory units, field trips, and work-study programs. Our impression, however, based on school observation and the research literature, is that there are two problems in this area. The first is the validity of the occupational sampling. For example, is a part-time position as a garage mechanic at the level of skill possessed by the student at that time a valid sampling of that occupation? Even if students perform skilled tasks (as opposed to menial tasks) — which is unlikely — they probably will not be responsible for customer relations or financial transactions and may not work the long hours of the regular staff. Is this a sufficient sampling?

More serious questions can be raised about talks by local employers and brief visits to local commercial, industrial, and professional establishments. In general, the provision of job-related experiences is of such high priority that the widest possible range of means should be employed including, for example, classroom career simulations.

The second problem is that of coordinating the experiences in such a way that they contribute significantly to the developing career plans of the students. Job-related experiences tend to be disconnected episodes without any cumulative influence on the students' developing plans, probably because students do not recognize the need to extract meaning from their experiences. Or, if they do recognize the need, they do not have the opportunity, the incentive, or the skill to initiate such activity. Furthermore, they may not receive the feedback on their performance in job-related experiences that is essential to the formulation and refinement of self-perceptions and career perceptions. This points to the fifth requirement of a comprehensive student guidance system.

Component 5.   Feedback and self-monitoring of career planning progress.

Students need feedback from the school and work environment on their progress in formulating appropriate plans and in acquiring the skills to implement them. This implies a carefully articulated sequence of experiences buttressed with a monitoring and information feedback system. In general, every career-relevant experience — throughout the students' high school experience — should be regarded as a significant informational input to their growing self-insight, occupational awareness, career exploration, and career progression. Students should receive feedback on their performance and the implications of that performance for subsequent planning. Career development through the high school years is — or should be — an iterative process of successive approximation whereby tentative plans are tested, reformulated, tested again, etc.

Component 6.   Procedures for group guidance and self-guidance.

In terms of traditional practices, this planning, testing, and reformulation would require conferences with a skilled counselor at frequent intervals. For a school on a two-semester plan, at least five conferences a year would be desirable: in the fall, after the start of the fall semester; at the end of the fall semester (to evaluate progress and to plan the spring semester); during the spring semester, and at the end of the spring semester — or during the summer — (to evaluate progress and plan the following year); plus an extra conference, assuming that some decisions would require two sessions, or interviews by the counselor with parents, teachers, and employers. Few high schools now have the guidance staff for such a schedule or are likely to have such staff in the foreseeable future. We estimate that to provide this degree of guidance service, one counselor would be required for every 180 students, and this staff would be necessary for career guidance alone. Thus, every effort must be made to make use of group guidance procedures, and to provide materials and equipment for self-instruction, self-planning, and self-exploration. The application of computer technology to this problem is by far the most promising possibility (see Chapter 6 for a detailed discussion). Several computerized interactive guidance systems are in advanced stages of development including information-processing systems by which a student can acquire feedback on his progress without assistance from a counselor or other school staff members. Such procedures are probably the main alternative to one-to-one counseling.

Students should be able to make decisions — about what courses to take, what occupational roles to sample through after-school employment, work-study programs, industrial arts and vocational courses, club activities, and summer jobs, and how much additional education to get—in the light of everything they know about themselves, what they want, their recent past experiences and the conclusions they drew from them, and the implications their decisions may have for future career options. Accordingly, the cumulative individual records should include entries summarizing the students' self-assessment and exploration along with the more formal academic indicators of their progress, such as academic grades and schoolwide achievement testing. Furthermore, the students need to have access to this cumulative record, quickly and inexpensively, whenever the need to make a particular decision arises. Thus, students need feedback on the results and implications of discrete experiences as well as cumulative data that will help them to evaluate the cumulative significance of their career exploration. If, for example, a student held a part-time position during the tenth grade and this position was a source of satisfaction and enlightenment to her or him, that information should be an element of the student's cumulative record, accessible to her or him when subsequent educational or vocational decision making is necessary. Use could be made of sophisticated information storage and retrieval systems, or a manual file system may be sufficient. (This operational problem will be discussed in Chapter 4).

Accumulated student career data of the type discussed is particularly useful to students who transfer to another high school, possibly in a distant location. How much of the student's cumulative record should be transferred and in what way (by the school, or by the student?) is a difficult question related to the sensitive issue of confidentiality. With the Buckley Amendment, the matter now has serious legal implications. Thus, this question will require extremely cautious and informed consideration. The simple alternative of wiping the slate clean each time the student transfers would not, we believe, be in the best interest of most students, although it might be for some.

In addition to accumulating data for the student's personal purposes, the school also needs certain student data for management and planning purposes and for fulfilling legal obligations to local, county, and state agencies. The relation between data keeping for student purposes and data keeping for school purposes is also discussed in Chapter 4.

Component 7. Access to a variety of types of information about the spectrum of occupations.

Implicit in all our remarks so far is the assumption that student acquisition of information about occupations is a high-priority outcome of elementary and secondary school education. Without this information, career planning is a vacuous—and even damaging—exercise, which may lead the student to premature commitment to educational and vocational pathways from which the student may not be able to switch without considerable loss of time. We have mentioned classroom and shop instruction and out-of-school experiences as sources of information about occupations. It is unlikely, however, that the student's need for occupational information can be fully met through these means. The pressures on the schools are great to teach students traditional knowledge and skills as well as more recently defined skills, such as safe driving. Contact hours in the classroom, laboratory, and shop are a precious commodity. Adding classroom instruction in decision making and the nature of occupations would place greater strains on the curriculum. There is therefore a pressing need for student initiative in acquiring this skill and understanding and for schools to provide the facilities and incentive to stimulate and expedite such self-learning. This need is widely recognized, but it is our observation that past efforts to satisfy it have met with limited success.

Judging from the reports of counselors and studies of student knowledge of occupations, students make limited use of the extensive files and libraries of occupational information available in their schools, and, when they do so, it is in a haphazard, unsystematic way. Two reasons may account for this limited use.

The first relates to the condition and the quality of the information itself, although many schools now have librarians solely for the maintenance of occupational literature. Most occupational libraries we have examined are so voluminous and so disorganized that locating the desired information requires hours of the student's time. Furthermore, the information itself is of spotty quality, frequently irrelevant to the student's needs, and often woefully outdated. At worst, it is prepared by partisan associations and commercial training schools with the objective of luring high school graduates into a particular trade or profession, presenting the student with a romanticized, sometimes inaccurate, picture of the occupation in question.

The second reason relates to student motivation to seek occupational information. Faced with the requirements of their classes and the demands of time-consuming extracurricular activities, few students are sufficiently motivated to take time for learning about occupations. Or, if they are motivated — as some surely are — they do not have the priority-setting skills to make the time available. Although most students probably recognize the need to learn about occupations, we think that the need is not given high priority in planning their daily schedules. The problem, here again, would seem to be one of confrontation and of helping students gain the planning and decision-making skills to enable them to achieve their objectives.

Although this analysis is conjectural and needs empirical investigation, we are confident that ready access to accurate, concise, and appealing occupational information is improving in some schools, but it remains a real need in many. As with other needs summarized in this section, it, too, is widely recognized. It is included here in the interest of completeness.

Also, in the interest of completeness, the widely recognized need for accurate information on supply and demand in the job market must be cited. This kind of information has at least two dimensions: geographical and temporal. In the case of the student who decides to seek employment immediately upon graduation, the need is primarily for knowledge of the likely local job market at the time of graduation, although it surely would be a mistake for students not to have access to five- or ten-year forecasts (as long as their fallibility is recognized).

For students who are considering careers which require higher education, the obvious need is for long-term national projections, such as those provided by the *Occupational Outlook Handbook*.

Component 8. Acquisition of decision-making skill.

All students are faced with a critical decision towards the end of high school in regard to their posthigh school educational and vocational involvements. Earlier in high school the emphasis is on planning and exploration. We reserve the term *decision making* for the kind of choice most students make at the end of high school. In part, this distinction between planning and decision making reflects our conviction that few, if any, students should commit themselves to a particular educational or career pathway early in high school. In exploration and planning, the emphasis is on strategies for acquiring self-insight, occupational information, and analytical skills, whereas in decision making the emphasis is on making choices.

This is not to say that planning does not involve decision making. It does indeed, and for this reason instruction in decision making cannot be postponed until late in high school.

Serious questions have been raised in the literature and by our colleagues about the effectiveness of teaching decision making, despite the existence and wide use of materials such as *Deciding* and *Decisions and Outcomes*, prepared by the College Board. We ask, however, why teaching this skill should, in principle, be any more difficult than teaching any complex cognitive skill. Students succeed in learning to solve difficult algebraic problems, to prove geometric theorems, to identify unknown chemicals, to unravel multicausation in the social sciences. Why, then, should they not be able to learn systematic, logical procedures for making personal decisions?

The acquisition of decision-making skill is, however, only half the battle, for there is an important difference between knowledge of decision making and the readiness to make decisions (Gribbons and Lohnes, 1968). A student may fully understand the mechanics of decision making yet be paralyzed when confronted with a critical choice. Readiness implies a kind of personal maturity not easily attained by any student, and perhaps never obtained by some. This suggests an interaction between personality development and career development that urgently needs investigation. If the materials now available to teach decision making are subject to criticism, it may be because they are too modest in their objectives. The acquisition of decision-making skill *and* the readiness to make career decisions may well require a carefully articulated program of instruction which continues throughout secondary school. This, in turn, will require that teachers receive advanced training in the complexities of decision making — training equivalent to that necessitated by the introduction of new approaches to science and mathematics instruction in the 1960s.

To the best of our knowledge, there have been no rigorous empirical demonstrations that instruction in decision making transfers to personal actions, in part because of the absence of suitable measures of this type of transfer. The development of suitable outcome or criterion measures in this area and their application in evaluative research should receive high priority.

Component 9. Interchangeability of educational pathways with minimal penalty to the student.

We have emphasized the need for early exploration and pre-liminary planning by the student, including the choosing of educa-tional pathways that are consistent with his or her plans, however tentative. In some high schools, this early choice of pathway will commit the student in undesirable ways, for in such schools there are barriers which make it difficult to switch to other pathways after the initial choice.

The barriers come in several forms, the main one being the fact that switching frequently requires the student to retrace his or her steps. A vocational student who decides to prepare for college may in some schools have to enroll in algebra I because the business mathematics course he or she took is not regarded as adequate prepa-ration for advanced mathematics or some science courses. Thus, a high school junior may have to be in a classroom of mostly ninth graders, a state of affairs which students tend to avoid if at all possible.

In the extreme, a student would have to repeat a whole year and as a consequence would need five years to complete high school, for most an even more unacceptable situation. Examination of 3,000 transcripts of graduating seniors in ETS's *Study of Academic Predic-tion and Growth* (referred to as the Growth Study) (Hilton et al., 1971) indicates that fewer than 1 percent of the graduates took more than four years to complete high school.

Exactly how constraining the high school curriculum structure and policies are requires further investigation and constitutes a high priority research item. For the purpose of this book, however, we will assume that the problem is real and that a fully effective guid-ance system must be designed to allow students to make tentative commitments without being locked into pathways difficult to re-verse. Possible steps to achieve this need consideration including curriculum revisions to facilitate switching from one pathway to another, provision of opportunities for the student to obtain the skills that are prerequisite to a particular pathway, and — most im-portant — steps to invalidate the concept that each and every student should complete high school in exactly four years.

There is ample research evidence that a large percentage of high school students — perhaps as many as 25 percent — have the ability to complete high school requirements in three years, whereas others could require five or six years to obtain minimal levels of compe-tency. If we add to this evidence the concept that for some students the high school experience should be one of study and extensive exploratory work experience (not merely summer positions and part-time work), the conclusion suggested is that it may be beneficial for some students to take even longer than five or six years to complete the requirements for graduation. It is critical, however, that the student perceive the extended study as desirable. In summary, secondary school education should not be regarded as having to fit into any particular block of time.

Component 10.   Assistance in financial planning.

An important component of a comprehensive system should be the availability of assistance in financial planning and possible financial aid so that no student should have to disrupt his or her education or be barred from an educational pathway solely for financial reasons. We recognize that a student may choose to interrupt his formal education for defensible personal reasons, but here we are referring to involuntary disruption which the student views as inimical to his or her career development.

We do not know what proportion of students now interrupt their high school education solely for financial reasons. If even a small percentage does — which seems likely — it is an unacceptable state of affairs. When it happens, the student should be encouraged, through the intervention of the guidance staff, to regard the disruption as temporary and as an opportunity to gain work experience which will contribute to his or her long-term career development.

As for financing post-high school education, the problem is twofold: identifying available financial resources, and apprising students of financial aids or low-cost educational alternatives (such as community colleges) that are available. Exactly how often students reject an appropriate post-high school pathway primarily for financial reasons is, to the best of our knowledge, unknown, but there are fragments of evidence that suggest the number is moderately large.

Component 11.   Comprehensive assessment of attainment in the senior year.

In the senior year the attainment of all students, whether they plan to continue their education or enter employment immediately upon graduation, should be comprehensively assessed. The assessment should take place in the late fall or early winter so that the results will be available for personal decision making in regard to job seeking or postsecondary schooling during the balance of the senior year. Although heavy reliance will continue to be placed on conventional pencil-and-paper objective tests, the assessment by no means needs to be restricted to these. Simulated tasks, oral examinations, performance ratings, and a number of other assessment techniques may well be more appropriate.

The assessment, which is already mandated in many states, has two main purposes: (1) to permit the school, the school district, and state agencies to evaluate the degree to which students have attained various educational objectives; and (2) to provide students with a comprehensive status report of their attainments to be used as a basis for judging whether they are, in fact, ready to terminate their secondary school education and, if so, as a basis for making plans for the period following high school.

Since students in many schools are repeatedly tested, for reasons not always apparent to the students, it is important that the assessment procedures be designed, as much as is possible, to make minimal demands on the students' time and be perceived by the students as a service to them. For example, the program planning and evaluation needs of the schools might be satisfied through matrix sampling, whereas the needs of individual students might be satisfied through longer tests or some other assessment technique administered on an optional basis.

Although it may not fully satisfy the purposes stated above, an alternative is a more flexible approach to attainment testing, conducted at whatever time a student appears to have mastered a particular competence. This alternative may also serve a diagnostic function particularly if the tests are designed in such a way that the scores suggest appropriate remedial action.

Who decides whether the student is ready to leave high school is a question requiring further consideration. Ideally, this judgment should be made by the student, provided he or she has attained some minimal degree of competency as defined, probably, by state legislatures. But we recognize that this ideal state presupposes a drastic change in how the function of the secondary school is perceived by students, parents, and school authorities. Specifically, it presupposes that high schools will come to be seen as a means for students to achieve the competencies which they need in the next step of their lives and that this step will be taken whenever the competencies are obtained regardless of how many (or few) semesters of study this attainment requires.

The competencies to which we refer are, indeed, comprehensive and include not only traditional academic and vocational skills, knowledge and understandings, but also skills in career planning, decision making, and interpersonal relations. Thus, we are allowing for the possibility that some students might choose to continue in high school because they have not as yet achieved the social and emotional maturity to cope effectively with the adult world. In the past, educators have argued against students leaving high school early—that is, after two or three years—on the grounds that most students need four years to achieve such maturity. We are suggesting that some students may need more than four years. The research evidence in this regard probably ought to be reexamined in the light of current educational developments.

In the traditional academic area, existing measurement procedures designed primarily for college admission are probably adequate for the kind of assessment proposed. Procedural changes—both administrative and financial—are necessary, however, when such testing of cognitive competencies is required of the student who does not plan to continue formal education immediately after graduation. Not to provide this assessment for students who will seek immediate employment deprives them of the opportunity to gain important self-insight—for possible future educational purposes—and deprives the school of the opportunity to assess the cognitive attainments of all its students.

It is widely recognized that measurement procedures beyond the traditional academic area are seriously deficient. For example, an acceptable, group-administered measure of motivation to continue learning simply does not exist. Measures of such attributes as attitude towards learning, artistic appreciation, self-insight, creativity, and self-esteem do exist, but most have characteristics which limit their general usefulness.

As for vocational competencies, group-administered measures suitable for the high school student are rare, judging from surveys of such instruments conducted at ETS (Boyd and Shimberg, 1971).

Just as students who will seek immediate employment should have the opportunity to assess their academic skills, so students who will continue their education should have the opportunity to assess their employability skills, although this might be optional. If such a student has, in one way or another, acquired unusual proficiency in, say, power mechanics and wishes this fact included in his or her permanent record, it should be possible to do so. Who knows, in this changing world, when the documentation might serve the student well? In general, along with many other contemporary writers (see, for example, Marland, 1970), we would endorse any steps that will destroy the concept that there are two kinds of high school students: academic and vocational.

We cannot leave this topic without acknowledging past criticism leveled against comprehensive senior-year test programs, such as the New York State Regents High School Examinations, on the grounds that they discourage innovation in the curriculum and influence teachers to "teach to the test." We see these outcomes as real dangers that cannot be belittled. Somehow the summarizing and reporting of results must be handled so as to minimize these undesirable side effects.

Component 12.   Aids and incentives for senior-year commitments.

For most students the crucial decision point and the one toward which much high school guidance effort is directed is the choice of a post-high school career pathway. In view of the widespread recognition of the importance of this decision, we need not belabor the point here. The current problem is that for all too many students the need for wise decision making is confronted for the first time at this point. If a comprehensive system functioned smoothly, post-high school choice would be a logical outcome of four to six years of planning and exploration rather than the uncertain and ego-rending experience it now is for so many students.

It is nonetheless true that students will always be faced with critical choices during the senior year. Well-advised students who are continuing their formal education will consider more than one appropriate school, that is, schools with programs consistent with their career plans, and will have to make a choice among those to which they are admitted.

Similarly, students seeking immediate employment will have to choose among jobs that are open to them. The need for accurate and up-to-date educational and occupational information is therefore more acute at this point than at earlier decision points.

Furthermore, it is crucial that by the senior year the students have acquired the skills to make the decisions they are confronted with. This is the payoff for the acquisition of systematic and effective decision-making skills gained prior to the senior year.

Component 13.   Assistance in job placement.

Students need information on the range of jobs which are available, as well as encouragement not to accept the first offer they may receive. For any one job opening they need the same kind of information and guidance they needed for prudent course selection: Where is the job likely to lead? What kind of knowledge and skills are required for successful performance on the job? What learning opportunities are there likely to be? Also what monetary and non-monetary rewards are likely to result and what costs will be incurred, such as union dues, purchase of uniforms and tools, commuting expenses, lost wages from shutdowns, bad weather, strikes, etc. The weights attached to these factors depend on the time horizon of the student. If the student sees a job as a long-term involvement rather than a short-term expedient, certain costs can be viewed as investments with long-term returns.

Component 14. Exit survey of career plans.

Just prior to graduation — during the last month of school if possible — each student in the graduating class should be surveyed in regard to post-high school plans. First, the survey should examine the degree of definiteness of the student's plans. For example, has the student made a tuition deposit to any school to which he or she has been admitted? Second, the specificity of the plans should be probed. If the student has made a commitment to attend a particular school, has he or she selected a program of study leading to a tentative career goal? Third, does the student have contingency plans in the event his or her primary plan changes or does not materialize? Fourth, the survey should reveal the time horizon of the student's plans. Has the student thought about the long-term implications of the plan, or has he or she been concerned only with the activities during the first year following graduation?

It is likely that some seniors will have been unable to settle on a career goal, despite honest efforts to do so. The high-ability student who has been consistently successful academically and in work-related activities might be an example. It is conceivable that such students have found no need for selecting a particular goal. At best they may only have excluded certain occupations from further consideration. For such students the school's role should be to guide them in formulating a strategy for selecting a career goal in the years immediately following high school. Such a strategy would require the identification of a number of educational or vocational options to be sampled, a sequential plan for doing so, and some thought about the basis on which the planned experiences will be evaluated. If a student without definite career goals has a planning strategy of this nature and also possesses the competencies, occupational knowledge, and decision-making skills to implement the strategy, we would regard him as a guidance success.

Component 15.   Posthigh school follow-up of each graduating class.

Essential to the continued operation and adjustment of a comprehensive guidance system is follow-up information from graduates. With this information the guidance staff can test its assumptions about the relationship between intentions or plans and actual posthigh school involvements.

A number of longitudinal studies have indicated that there is extensive slippage between plans and actual posthigh school activities. Typically, a substantial percentage of the students who indicated they planned to attend four-year colleges actually enrolled in two-year colleges or obtained immediate employment; a somewhat larger percentage who indicated they planned to obtain immediate employment actually continued their education. Current data on this question is available from the first follow-up of the *National Longitudinal Study of the High School Class of 1972* (Tabler, 1976).

Since the slippage varies from one high school to another, it is necessary for each high school to conduct its own follow-ups. Ideally both one-year and five-year follow-ups are desirable, for longitudinal studies have shown that the correlation between status of students one year after graduation and their status five years after graduation is far less than one. The pattern of migration from each educational or occupational status to others during the years immediately following graduation is information essential for curriculum planning and guidance. If, for example, 75 percent of the students who attend two-year colleges subsequently graduate from four-year colleges, the implications for guidance are quite different from what they would be if 75 percent of the students who graduate from two-year colleges seek immediate employment. Similarly, if, one year after graduation, the majority of the graduates of a particular vocational program are working at jobs which are related to their training but five years later the majority are employed in positions requiring other skills, the information would have critical implications for curriculum planning.

An elaborate questionnaire is not necessary for these purposes. One page, or even a return postcard, should be sufficient. Other shortcuts, like sampling of the graduates, also can reduce the expense of the task. Some local schools may need assistance in instrument design, sampling techniques, and data analysis. This could be an important role for state agencies.

These, then, are what we see as the 15 critical components of secondary school career guidance. How these components can be integrated into a comprehensive system is discussed in the next two chapters, first at an abstract level and then, in Chapter 4, in more operational terms.

CHAPTER 3

A Conceptual Model of the Student Development Process during High School[1]

Underlying the foregoing enumeration of the components of a comprehensive high school guidance system is a conceptualization of the guidance process that we should now like to make explicit. In our conceptualization, using the language of information processing, we will view the student as a complex information processing system exposed over time to a barrage of informational inputs from the environment. The student receives and processes the information in the same way that a computer responds to data inputs and programed instructions from the environment. But, unlike conventional computers (except for experimental devices being developed in research settings), the student is transformed by the experience. In other words, the student comprehends and learns. After this experience, the student is a different and more capable information-processing system.

Moreover, unlike computers, students have control over their environment. They can select what inputs they will expose themselves to and, in a given situation, what inputs they will pay attention to, and — sometimes to their detriment — what inputs they will disregard. Ultimately, students can transform their environment and,

1. In this chapter more than in others, we have drawn on the ideas of guidance theorists of the past 20 or 30 years. We cannot list all to whom we are indebted, but we would be unforgivably remiss if we did not acknowledge the contributions of Donald E. Super and David V. Tiedeman. In a very real way our conceptualizing has consisted of a rediscovery of their pathfinding work.

through their initiative, make it a better environment for their development. Students can, for example, take steps to improve the quality of instruction they receive. Thus, we view students as complex information processors — not passive recipients of information but active agents of their individual progress, or capable of becoming so.

THE GENERAL MODEL

In thinking about the development of a student through high school and afterwards, we have asked what the major informational inputs are, what major processes take place, and what the outcomes of these processes are. A simplified schematic representation of student development viewed in this way is shown in Figure 1. In this diagram and those that follow, the dotted-line boxes indicate information sources or statuses and the solid-line boxes indicate processes. Beginning at the left, we show the student at entry into high school. The major informational input to the high school experience is Student History. (The term *history* is used as a brief description of a broad range of student attributes including traits, values, beliefs, needs, skills, knowledge, and memories.) To predict the outcomes of the high school experience, at least two other informational inputs are necessary. The first is the kind of educational treatments to which he is exposed. "Educational treatments" include the teaching techniques and personality of the teacher, the teaching materials, the physical aspects of the classroom, laboratory or shop, and any other situational variables that influence learning. Since the mix of treatments a particular student is exposed to depends primarily on what courses or subjects the student selects (or is assigned to), we have shown Course Selections as the first additional input. The second major input consists of the School, Family, Peer, and Community variables that influence the outcome of the educational process.

As a result of the high school learning experience, the students achieve a certain exit status, different from their entry status. For our present purposes, the ingredient of most interest is their competencies. But to predict the outcome of high school experience, that is, how they function after high school, we need to know, first, what kind of post-high school educational and occupational situations they enter. Simplifying a vastly complex process, the diagram shows this informational input simply as Career Plans, but their be-

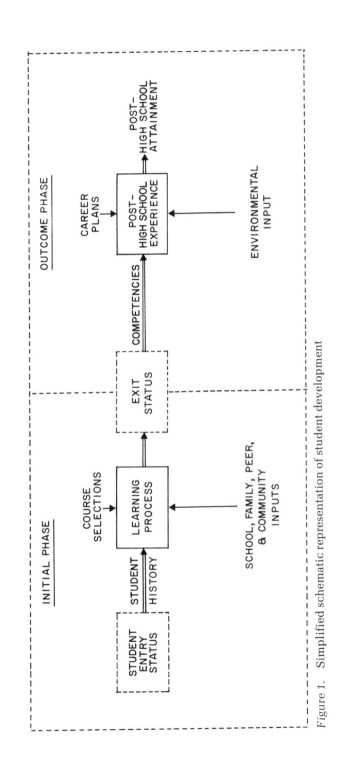

Figure 1. Simplified schematic representation of student development

havior after high school also depends on a myriad of environmental inputs (job opportunities, educational opportunities, the state of the economy, family support, etc.). These environmental variables interact with the competencies that the students bring to their post-high school life, as selected in accordance with their career plans, and result in certain post-high school attainment.

DEVELOPMENT IN THE TRADITIONAL SCHOOL

To simplify subsequent diagrams we have divided Figure 1 into two phases, Initial and Outcome. To further simplify this exposition, let us first consider student development in the traditional high school. Whether the school depicted exists now, or ever did exist, is not crucial to our argument.

The critical question in our hypothetical traditional school is where Course Selections come from. Figure 2, a schematic representation of this process, focuses only on the initial phase of Figure 1. As shown at the right of the diagram, we are hypothesizing that the first ingredient of course selection is student performance data, which are evaluated by the faculty. The grades are transmitted to a record file maintained by the guidance department. Subsequently the grades and information about the high school curriculum are given to parents, from which they form judgments about course selection. These judgments, grades, and counselor recommendations are the major informational inputs to the course selection process. In theory, counselors only make recommendations, to help students make their own decisions. Our observation, however, is that contemporary guidance counselors, typically overloaded, have greater influence on student decision making than guidance texts would recommend. In any case, the outcome is an academic or vocational program for the student to follow in the next semester. This process is repeated each semester or, in some schools, annually, until graduation.

An exception to this process occurs prior to the first semester of high school, when course selection is also influenced by the student's prehigh school records, for example, test scores, grades, teacher anecdotal reports, as shown at the lower left of Figure 2.

As for the processes of the Outcome Phase (see Figure 3), the key box is in the center, labeled Student Decision Making. We are hypothesizing that decision making is based on six major informational inputs:

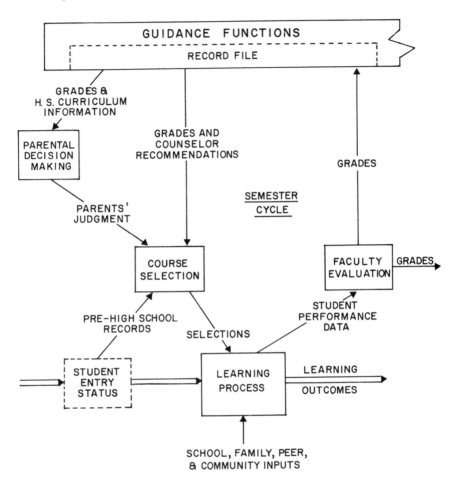

Figure 2.   Initial phase of student development in traditional school

1. *Emotions and beliefs.* Included are feelings, notions, and
    impressions — conscious and unconscious — about occupa-
    tions, beliefs about careers and what is expected of oneself.
    (The connotation of nonrationality in our choice of words is
    intentional.)

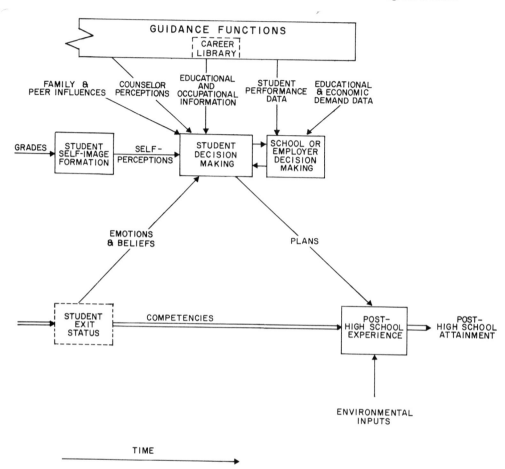

Figure 3.   Outcome phase of student development in traditional high school

2. *Self-perceptions.* These perceptions, we hypothesize, result
from a self-image formation process, in which academic
grades form a major input. Counselors, teachers, peers, and
the student's family also influence self-image formation,
especially during earlier years, but our hypothesis is that
these influences — while important — are not as great during
the secondary school years as traditional academic grades.
This is an area that urgently needs empirical study. Coleman's work (1961) is highly relevant.

3. *Family and peer influences.* These have a direct bearing on student decision making in the traditional high school.
4. *Counselor perceptions.*
5. *Educational and occupational information.* The extent to which this information influences students in the traditional high school depends on its accessibility and quality and on the students' readiness to make decisions.
6. *Decision making by the schools and employers.* Student decision making is bilateral. The plan which a student decides upon depends on decisions made by schools to which he or she applies for admission or by employers to which he or she applies. In turn, the judgments of these decision makers are influenced by informational inputs received from the schools. Thus, according to this model, student performance affects student decision making in two ways: through its effect on the decision making by schools and employers, and through its effect on the formation of student self-image.

DEVELOPMENT IN PROPOSED SCHOOL

So far, we have focused on our impression of student development in the traditional high school, primarily as a way of illustrating our general approach to the student development process. The schematic representations also serve as a baseline for the developmental processes of the proposed comprehensive guidance system.

Basically, the proposed system is not radically dissimilar from the traditional system. It departs from the traditional system in three major ways. (1) Students would assume a central role in evaluating their progress, in formulating strategies for developing career plans, and in deciding which courses and what related experiences they will involve themselves in. (2) To assume that central role, students would have more access to information about their personal characteristics, their performance, and the occupational and educational environment. (3) Guidance functions would be substantially broadened. At the risk of great oversimplification, we would characterize the traditional career counselor as a gatekeeper, record keeper, and purveyor of information. Characterizing our proposed counselor is not as easy. Perhaps something like *student development specialist* describes their new role as collaborators with the instructional staff in arranging learning experiences, as specialists in the assessment of student characteristics and broad educational outcomes, as specialists in information processing, storage, and retrieval, and finally, as experts in facilitating student decision making.[2]

Remember that our traditional school may be a complete anachronism. We recognize that many components of our proposed system are now in place in schools throughout the country. We hope some readers will find comfort in knowing that they have been doing for a long time what we propose here.

The initial phase of student development for the proposed system is shown in Figure 4. Although the general outline is the same as Figure 2, it differs in subtle but important ways. The first change is the addition of the phase labeled Reformulation of Strategies by the Student. At the end of each semester, the student's performance is reviewed and evaluated by the student and by others (instructors, counselors, employers, coaches, club advisors). Some part of this evaluation becomes part of the accumulated record, ideally to be maintained by the students themselves. Other parts of the evaluation go to the school's data file, not necessarily in the form of traditional academic grades. (What information should be stored and in what form obviously need further study.) Most important, the outcome of this evaluation becomes a basis for reformulation or refinement by the students of their strategies for gaining career awareness and self-insight. On the basis of this reformulation, the students, with whatever assistance they may need, plan which educational and work-related experiences they wish to be involved in during the next semester. Parents will participate in this planning, but not as primary decision makers who form judgments on the basis of academic grades received from the guidance office. Double arrows connect Parent Participation and Planning by Students to emphasize the desired two-way communication between parents and students. We have deliberately not shown input arrows directly from the guidance department to each process, to emphasize the importance of the student as the central figure in the planning process. "Counselor Inputs" is diagramed as influencing the total development process rather than any one aspect of the process.

A second change is that data from the school files are available to the student and to the staff (with the possible exception of certain

2. A similar conception of the career guidance counselor was presented by Shertzer and Stone (1974).

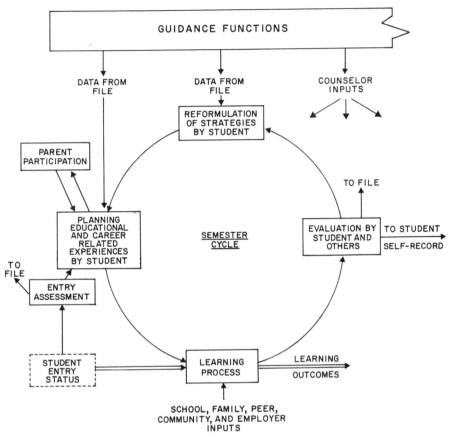

Figure 4.   Initial phase of student development in proposed system

data such as medical records which have confidential status as far as some parties are concerned) but only when called for by the person needing the information. In general, it is our conviction that individual decision making should never be constrained or influenced by the manner in which personal data are stored, processed, or made available to the decision maker.

A third feature of the proposed system is Entry Assessment in which the entry characteristics of the students are comprehensively assessed in a standardized manner. (Some steps to develop the measures that this will require are proposed in Chapter 6.) The

purposes of such assessment are, first, to facilitate rational planning by the students and, second, to obtain baseline measurement for
the kind of program evaluation described in subsequent chapters.

The outcome phase of the proposed system is shown in Figure 5.
Note that we have omitted the schools or employers as decision
makers who have a major immediate influence on the career plans
of the students. This, again, is to dramatize the central role of the
students as the principal architects of their future. We would hope
(but recognize it may represent more of a goal than a short-term
realization) that the students of the future will be so self-motivated
and so well equipped, well informed, and versatile that the availability of a particular educational or vocational option will not be a
major element in their decision making. Such students will create
options rather than passively respond to them.[3] Note also that exit
assessment is added (Comprehensive Terminal Assessment) both as
an input to student decision making and as an ingredient of program
evaluation (To File). A provision for follow-up data (Follow-up
Survey) is also added.

Another subtle but significant change is the new role of the student as the influencer of environmental inputs. We are proposing
that students not only determine which posthigh school pathway
they will follow but also that active assertive students can influence
the kind of inputs they receive from the environment. Once in a
pathway, by virtue of the posthigh school choice they make, they
can select options (such as academic majors, part-time study, departments or specialties within an organization, leisure-time activities) that will contribute to further career exploration or to refinement of their plans or to the attainment of their career goals or
further self-insight (or "all of the above").

Next, we would point to the self-image formation process. In the
proposed system, the major input is not grades but all the recorded
insights accumulated through the high school years, including, but
by no means limited to, academic grades.

Counselor Perceptions are omitted on the grounds that what
counselors think students ought to do—for example, which schools
they ought to apply to—will not be *primary* considerations in student decision making. Students will consult counselors and teachers,
whose role will be to facilitate decision making, not to shape it.
Family influences remain in the model, as a reflection of the authors'

---

3. Sprinthall's (1971) view of the goal of guidance is relevant here.

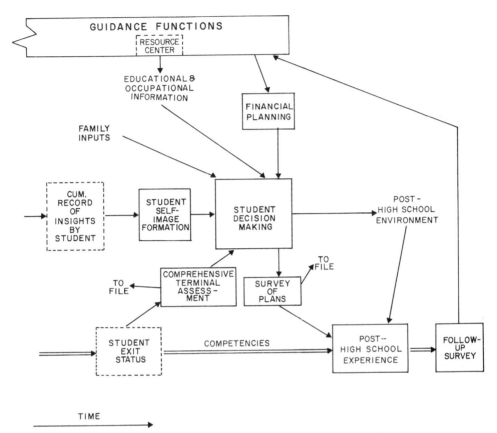

Figure 5.   Outcome phase of student development in proposed system

expectation that there will continue to be a correlation between the occupations of parents and the occupation of their offspring, if only for economic reasons. A higher proportion of the children of physicians will become physicians than the children of farmers, and vice versa.

Peer inputs, however, are omitted as a primary influence. This omission reflects our perception that peers are frequently a source of misinformation and inexpert advice. Peers may always be a major influence, however, and if students of the future are knowledgeable about occupations and decision making, it may not be an undesirable state of affairs.

Finally, there is the addition of financial planning information, contributing more directly than in the traditional system to student decision making, either when students interrupt their high school education prior to graduation or when they plan their post-high school experience.

To show the total system, Figure 6 combines Figures 4 and 5 into one diagram. Although complicated enough, this schematic representation does not convey the many interactions among the people involved or the scope of the larger educational setting in which it is imbedded. These topics are discussed in the next chapter along with some considerations about how the total system might actually operate.

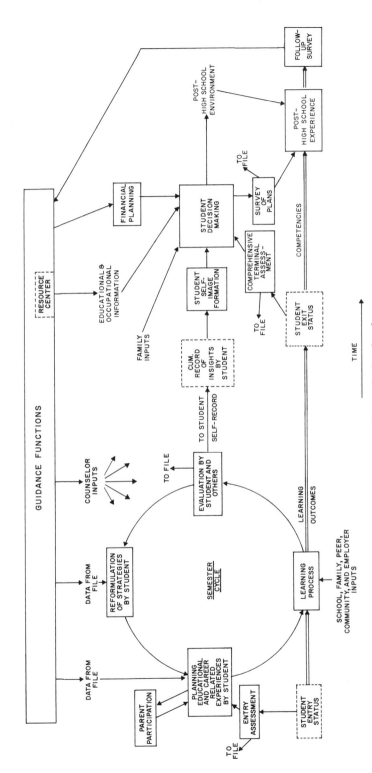

Figure 6.   Conceptualization of student development process during high school

The School and Its Staff — Crucial Elements of the Comprehensive Career Guidance System

The implementation of a comprehensive career guidance system of the kind described in the preceding chapters will have a great impact on the entire school system and on the community. The functions, roles, and relationships among administrators, teachers, guidance personnel, students, parents, and members of the community will change during this process of beginning a new system of guidance. To convey our perception of the change that may take place, we will first discuss briefly the total school system in which the comprehensive system is imbedded, and then we will present a more specific chronological overview of the way in which the particular system that we have proposed might function.

THE ROLES IN A TRADITIONAL SCHOOL SYSTEM

Let us first consider a brief description of a traditional school system, acknowledging in the beginning that the description is oversimplified and overdrawn in order to highlight its basic elements. Our intent is not to demean any of the crucial roles in the educational process, but rather to describe the basic elements and relationships of a traditional system in such a way that the contrasts with the proposed system are quite clear. As with the traditional school described in Chapter 3, the traditional system that we describe here may be a complete anachronism.

In this traditional system, the roles of school administrators, teachers, guidance personnel, students, parents, and intermediate- or state-level officials are quite well defined. The roles are compartmentalized, and interaction among the participants is limited. The school administrators have high status. Their major contacts are with each other, the school board, and intermediate-unit or state officials. Less frequently, they work with teachers except during the initial phases and planning of the curriculum or development of new curriculums, and during collective bargaining and grievance proceedings. Their contacts with guidance personnel and students are even rarer and occur primarily when there are student disciplinary problems. All too often they perceive their role as "running the school," not as helping the students to achieve specified objectives.

The teachers occupy the next rank in the hierarchy. Their primary contacts are with the students and with each other; much less frequently do they deal with the administrators or the guidance staff. Their role is generally limited to providing conventional courses of instruction, and to teaching academic or vocational skills. Many high school teachers see their role solely as preparing the student for further educational experiences.

Even in an oversimplified account, it is difficult to categorize the guidance staff in the traditional school. They do not have the power or authority of the administrators, and yet they are not always accepted as professional equals by members of the teaching staff. In some schools, however, they are seen as being in a favored position. Frequently, members of the guidance staff perceive their positions as a stepping stone to administrative-level positions. Their contacts with teachers and administrators on a continuing basis tend to be minimal. As for contacts with students, in many schools a one-to-one relationship for one of two specific purposes is their primary contact — either to assist the students in setting up schedules or resolving schedule conflicts, or to assist students in college placement.

In our hypothetical traditional school, the students are often viewed by administrators, teachers, and guidance staff as children ("kids") to be directed through the high school process in a specified time (four years) with as few problems as possible. Many students themselves perceive the high school period as a sentence to be endured, either as a prerequisite to college or as a period they must survive because the law says so. Too few students see the period or process as one that is personally meaningful, a period during which significant personal goals can be established and achieved. The students typically meet with teachers only in the classroom situation, where interaction consists of acquiring specific knowledge or academic skills. For most students the only other interaction with school personnel is with the guidance staff, although here, too, the specific objectives are usually limited — setting up the next semester's schedule or choosing their next school. The typical student rarely interacts with administrators except in disciplinary matters.

The role of parents varies. Some have little or no contact with the teachers, the administrators, or the guidance staff except for an occasional back-to-school night or for a disciplinary problem. Others are so intensely involved with their children during this process that they dominate the situation to the detriment of the student. Still others abdicate their responsibility to the "school." Probably the most numerous are those parents who have a real interest and a desire to be helpful to their children, but who lack the initiative and/or knowledge to interact effectively with the many kinds of individuals concerned with the entire process.

Finally, there are the intermediate-unit and state-level educational officials, who interact almost exclusively with each other and with the local school administrators. Their relationship with the local school administrators tends to be largely one-way — they receive reports from the local level, the substance of which is primarily financial or statistical, or they issue policy statements and directives that are the result of legislative action.

The information system that supports the operation of the traditional, conventional school system has two significant characteristics. First, the information tends to be highly compartmentalized — staff members maintain separate information files to suit their own needs, and there is relatively little sharing of information between, for instance, teachers and guidance staff. Second, the focus is very much on information about, not for, the students. Except for grade records and attendance report files, information is collected and maintained *about* the student without being fed back to the student.

ROLES IN THE PROPOSED SCHOOL SYSTEM

In the proposed system, many components of which are already in effect in varying degrees throughout the United States today, the first objective is to aid *all* students to develop appropriate and

realistic plans for their careers in the period following high school;
the second objective is to equip students with the skills and knowledge necessary to enable them to implement their plans effectively.
Achieving these objectives requires changes in the roles and relationships among the staff, as well as a reformulation of the information system.

The Role of the Administrator

Of all the roles in the proposed system, the administrator's is
perhaps less changed from the traditional model than are the other
roles. The administrators continue to meet their usual financial and
managerial responsibilities, but in addition they assume a more active role as change agents in supporting the integration of the teaching and guidance functions and in developing significantly higher
levels of community involvement. The proposed system rests to a
larger degree on new teaching and guidance roles and on a closer
integration of these functions. To achieve these changes, the administrative staff supports strongly both the stated objectives and the
processes and procedures necessary to achieve the objectives. It is
the administrators, for example, who use their contacts and skills to
increase the involvement of local employers in the development and
implementation of an appropriate career guidance program for the
school. By their positive support, the administrators play a key role
in introducing heretofore nonstandard educational experiences.
Furthermore, the positions of the administrators enable them to
convince the various publics — school board, parents, and taxpayers
— of the benefits of full participation in the student career guidance
system. In such systems, the administrators have significantly increased interaction with the teachers and guidance staff about substantive educational issues.

The Role of the Guidance Staff

Perhaps the most radical and comprehensive role and relationship changes occur in the guidance function. The distinctions between teaching staff and guidance staff will diminish as each assumes more responsibility for students' career development. More
than other staff members, the guidance staff function as catalysts
and coordinators of a social system that involves as active participants in the process the teachers, students, parents, and employers
in the community. Although the guidance staff may spend less time

working with individual students, their impact on the students increases as a result of their active interaction with the teachers and administrators.

Precisely how classroom teachers and career guidance counselors divide responsibility and resolve any role conflicts is an unanswered question. Patterns probably vary from one school to another, as they always have. We can only be sure that, in the proposed school, teachers and counselors are partners in stimulating students to:

1. Engage in positive self-confrontation.
2. Obtain and use information pertaining to careers, occupations, and employment trends.
3. Develop strategies and skills for career decision making.
4. Create career plans and evaluate the adequacy of such plans.

In addition, teachers and counselors collaborate in creating courses that contain career-relevant elements. From examples of the ways in which various occupations and careers use or require certain academic and vocational skills and knowledge, the student gains a broader information base about a variety of careers.[4]

Working closely with administrators and teachers, the guidance staff also develops work-related experience programs in cooperation with local employers and community leaders. Such programs, where students gain exposure to a variety of occupations, are an important aspect of the proposed system even though there are problems in making the programs as valuable as they might be. The guidance staff acts as coordinators and facilitators between the teaching staff and employers in planning the work experiences that can be incorporated into the curriculum without reducing the quality of the academic work, and in designing the work sampling experiences that are significant and comprehensive.

The guidance staff's relationship with students is also significantly different from that found in the conventional school setting. Rather than functioning primarily as problem solvers for students, the guidance personnel are the implementers and managers of the student career guidance system. They teach students how to make the guidance system and its components work for them. Rather than providing answers for students, they aid the students in the use of

4. Relevant additional discussion of the new role of guidance can be found in Herr and Cramer (1972).

their own resources and the resources of the system to answer their questions. In this role the guidance staff has a key responsibility for helping the students move from being a directed element to becoming a directing agent in career development. Only in this way can a student learn to function in a self-directed manner in the world beyond high school.

Creating a climate where confrontation, exploration, and reformulation of ideas and plans are not only accepted but are encouraged is a difficult task, particularly in schools where there are strong historical precedents for choosing an educational pathway at the beginning of the process (usually in the ninth grade) and then following it through to the end. More and more schools are offering curriculums that give students an opportunity to explore multiple educational options prior to choosing a pathway that will be followed through grade 12. (As early as the 1940s some schools—Montclair, New Jersey, for example—had a core and elective form of curriculum, without separate tracks for different programs, and in Illinois and other midwestern states in the early 1950s the "core curriculum" plan was being tried in numbers of schools.)

The idea of encouraging students to question their professed goals and the implications of their educational accomplishments is one which many students and school staff instinctively regard with concern, even anxiety. Confrontation, though it has a negative connotation, may be the most effective means of achieving in students a level of awareness, self-knowledge, and motivation needed for effective career decision making. To see this as a positive and helpful process, however, the students need strong and continuous training, support, and encouragement from the guidance and teaching staffs. Without such training, it is not easy for students to review objectively their tentative career goals and assess their own willingness to attain the skills necessary to reach those goals. Without such support, it is not easy for students to shift from one educational path to another and to face the consequent disapproval of their parents, friends, and the school staff, who may regard them as indecisive and time-wasting.

The Role of the Teaching Staff

As a first step in the proposed approach, teachers must review and revise curriculums from a new point of view, namely, to facilitate career development. While it remains important that curricu-

lums and course sequences reflect certain subject-matter requirements, it is also important that teachers play a central role in
designing curriculums in which students can explore the widest
variety of academic fields in the minimum amount of time as well
as avoid any loss of time because of changes in educational pathways. To achieve this, initial or introductory courses are designed to
provide an overview of a field or discipline for the exploring student
and also to serve as the background course for students who choose
at a later time to pursue the field more extensively.

Courses later in the curriculum are designed to facilitate and
capitalize upon occupational sampling activities. This implies more
modular courses that students can enter and leave at a number of
break points, but in which the academic quality of the course is
maintained.

Teachers also try to increase the career-related aspects and relevance of the courses to help students meet the career guidance objectives. In many instances teachers accomplish this by making more
extensive use of examples from various occupations as specific skills
and concepts are taught and by asking business and professional
leaders in the community to teach special segments of courses. This
not only provides greater opportunities for the students to learn
firsthand about various occupations and careers, but also increases
the involvement and participation among those professional, industrial, and commercial people of the community who are essential to
the functioning of the external occupational sampling program.

Perhaps the most significant change in the teacher's role occurs
as the teacher becomes more involved in the career guidance process.
Currently, the lack of enough guidance staff is commonly lamented.
It is ironic that members of the teaching staff, a group of highly
trained personnel, typically spend much more time with students
than the guidance staff does, yet, except on an occasional and informal basis, teachers do not assist students in career planning and
decision making. In the proposed system, the differences between
teaching and guidance staffs become less distinct since the teaching staff, with appropriate training from the guidance staff, begin to
assume a planned, active role in the career development of students.

It is obvious that any career guidance system cannot be fully
effective without human interaction at certain points. It is important
to develop the student's abilities to record information, make plans,
and evaluate and revise them, but the system would be sterile indeed
(and of questionable effectiveness) if there were no significant hu-

man intervention. Even students who may most jealously guard their privacy come to a point where they find it crucial to discuss their plans, hopes, and concerns with another person who knows them and has an interest in them. At this point, both counselors and teachers can make an invaluable contribution to the student's development.

The Role of Parents and the Community

With parents, the issue of interaction is particularly important yet difficult to manage because, in the laboratory sense, the parents represent an uncontrollable variable in the process. Although it would be difficult, if not impossible, to build a system that copes effectively with parents who are either extremely dominating or extremely uninvolved, the proposed system is aimed at the many parents in the middle category who would like to be helpful but do not know how.

An objective of the proposed system is to have parents gain an understanding about the process and a knowledge of the school personnel that enable them to contribute their unique knowledge and insights in a positive and supportive manner to the student. Effective communication from the school is needed to achieve this objective. For instance, the parents understand that the students maintain their own information file (the Student Log), which they may not choose to share (at least completely) with them. The parents should come to understand that such behavior is normal, not indicative of a problem between the parents and student, and is, in fact, essential to the development of a self-reliant individual.

Local business and professional people provide another human resource that enriches the curriculums and at the same time demonstrates the relevance and importance of the secondary school experience to the students. As with the parents, it is essential that the cooperation of this group be obtained and that they understand the program; otherwise, the program suffers from the lack of career-sampling opportunities.

The Role of Intermediate and State Agencies

Educational officials at the intermediate and state levels continue their essential role as receivers of various kinds of statistical and financial information from the local districts and as communicators of legislatively derived policy in the proposed system, but an additional, critical information-processing function is added.

In the proposed system, most of the information is processed not about, but for, the student. An important element in this store of information for the student concerns occupational needs and trends. This information about short-term and long-term supply and demand data is crucial for the student who is exploring the potential in various occupations and careers. The information pertains to several levels — local, regional, state, and national.

The intermediate and state officials are responsible for the collection, validation, and dissemination to the local school system of the occupational information described above. By serving as a coordination and control point, these officials ensure that the information being utilized by students across the state is accurate and comparable. In fulfilling this role, the state officials work with intermediate unit officials, with officials in adjacent states, and with federal agencies to compile and disseminate regional, state-level, and national information.

INFORMATION REQUIREMENTS OF THE PROPOSED SYSTEM

Our discussion of the proposed information system covers (1) the objectives that the system is designed to meet, (2) several significant design requirements or constraints that are necessary if the context and assumptions considered in the design of the system are to be understood, and (3) the structure of the system in nontechnical terms.

The general objective of the information system is twofold: to facilitate the students' learning, inquiry, assessment, and decision-making processes that are prerequisites to making appropriate and satisfying career choices; and to support the schools' responsibilities for operating, monitoring, and evaluating the student career-guidance system. Within this general objective are more specific objectives that pertain to the students, school systems, and intermediate units or states.

For the student the objective is to collect, process, retain, analyze, and present student-generated information with appropriate contextual information supplied by the school, the state, and other sources.

For the school system the three objectives are to present to the student information from local, regional, state, and national sources; to collect and analyze student data for purposes of monitoring the operation of the student career-guidance system and of evaluating its effectiveness at the school level; and to provide the necessary inputs for processing and analysis at the intermediate or state level.

At the state level there also are three objectives. The first is the crucial input function — that of collecting, coordinating, controlling, and disseminating to the local school systems information from the state, regional, and national levels that concerns careers and employment trends, as well as current and projected statistical data necessary for the functioning of student career guidance; the control aspect of this function is especially important since the inclusion of inappropriate or conflicting data or the absence of data in the system would create serious problems for the students. The second objective is to collect data from the school system for continuing state level ad hoc analyses that aid in evaluating the impact and effectiveness of the system and that support the study of policy issues at the state level. The third objective is to provide such state-wide information as is required at the federal level.

The proposed information system calls for several important design requirements or constraints. First, although automated processing is a requirement for certain aspects of the system, the system must be able to operate effectively at the student and school levels with considerable variation in the amount and kinds of automated processing support.

Second, the system must be designed in such a way that information at the student level can — at the option of the student — be kept confidential from all other users of the system. This is an interesting and challenging requirement, since it reverses the usual confidentiality requirement of other information management systems.

Third, the system must accommodate intermittent processing at the student level to achieve the most highly personalized environment possible, without unduly affecting the efficiency of the scheduled, cyclical processing required at the school and state levels. Finally, the system should require a minimum of initial training and be easy for students to operate. More rigorous training and operational requirements are allowable at the school and state level.

Figure 7 shows the relationships between the student subsys-

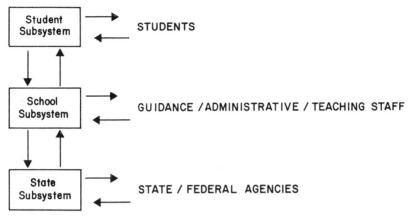

Figure 7.   Career guidance information system

tem, the school subsystem, the state subsystem and the various users of the system. Information flows are indicated by the arrows.

The Student Subsystem

In an ideal system, virtually all the information processing could and would be automated. To require such extensive automation, however, would ignore the technological, economic, and staffing realities that exist today in education and that are likely to continue for the indefinite future. Therefore, the conceptualization is drawn so that it is not essential for the subsystem to be completely automated, and the description of the student subsystem is couched for the most part in neutral terms. It is likely, in an implementation of the system, that the greatest part of the information processing in this subsystem would not be automated. Practical considerations might well dictate this rule: automate only when no other way can accomplish the function effectively.

The student's initial contact with the system is in an input mode. The student establishes his or her existence and identity with the information processing system. The student then begins to record extensive personal information: background, environment, and plans and goals even though it may perhaps be poorly formulated at this time. This initial record or picture of the student can contain elements that he or she chooses never to share with others. Here strict confidentiality must be maintained at the lowest levels of data aggregation.

An important distinction must be drawn here. Certain personal information, likely to be largely unquantifiable, may be recorded and retained by the student and never shared. This record will serve to remind the student of possibly significant experiences when the need to make choices arises later. Other personal or sensitive data would never be released by the system on an individual or personal basis; however, these data may be collected and released as summary data at the school and state levels, where they are a necessary input for the operation and evaluation of the career guidance system.

Beyond the initial data entry phase, the student continuously records data about his or her plans (new and revised), activities, accomplishments, perceptions, and opinions. The information is recorded and retained in a manner that facilitates the student's continuing self-analysis. During the cyclical process the student may be motivated to ask for assistance from the guidance/teaching staff and, as he or she feels it appropriate to do, share with them the information recorded. Obviously, students must realize that the understanding and support of the career guidance counselors, their teachers, and their parents are essential in this process.

Periodically the student is required to put into the system information about his or her status in the process, so that the system can provide the student with information about his or her progress or lack of progress and can feed necessary operational control information to the school subsystem.

Other data are also introduced into the processing system in order to prepare more sophisticated individual analyses for the student. For example, the student provides information about his or her interests, tentative career plans, and present educational plans and achievements. The system compares this pattern or picture with other individual and aggregate data to give the student a quantified, objective assessment of the "goodness of fit" between his or her career plans, identified interests, educational program, and achievements. The student can share such an individual analysis, if he or she chooses. Within the system, however, the information is used by others only if the individual identification is deleted.

The issue of confidentiality cannot be overemphasized in the student subsystem. For the subsystem to be effective, the students must perceive it as a totally private extension of their own intellectual resources and must fully understand what information is shared and how identification of the individual is protected.

A possible exception to the confidentiality is for counselors to be informed when programed decision rules identify students who are in need of follow-up because of a confusion about plans, the inaccurate use of the system, or discrepancies between their personal history and their plans. In such cases, counselors can at least volunteer their assistance. Without assistance, students may make decisions on the basis of inaccurate information and perceptions. Clearly, many details of this proposed system remain to be worked out, and controlled experiments need to be conducted to identify the most effective variations.

The School Subsystem

Much of the information processing in this subsystem is automated. The bulk of the input to this subsystem comes from the individual student subsystem. These data are processed in such a way as to make the administration of the career-guidance system feasible. Of primary importance is the implementation of an "exception reporting principle" in the control aspects of this system, mentioned above. A computer run might identify a group of students who earlier had expressed an interest in engineering as a career, but who currently are not studying mathematics. A difficult but important function of the guidance staff is the development of decision rules that determine what kind of information they receive, and when. Such decision rules probably should be subject to review by the faculty and administrative staff.

Student data without individual identification are analyzed to provide both the guidance/teaching and administrative staffs with the information required to evaluate the effectiveness of the system at the school system level. As a result of such evaluations, local changes are instituted and/or suggestions for change passed on to the state level. The processed information at this level (both status and substantive) in turn becomes input data to the state subsystem.

The State Subsystem

The initial function of this subsystem, the information processing of which is the one most likely to be automated, is the collection of the nonstudent input data needed at the school level. It is necessary for this function to be very carefully planned and controlled. All the employment and career information from the many state and federal agencies that supply such material is funneled through this system at the state level. Without careful and thorough control at the state level, the student subsystems within a state suffer greatly from a lack of uniform, accurate, and appropriate information. Theoretically, it might be ideal to have this control exercised at the federal level; in practice, however, it would appear that the state level yields the necessary control and still allows for a timely flow of information.

The second major function is the processing of the aggregate school district data to provide state level summary reports. These reports both serve the system's administrative requirements at the state level and provide the basis for necessary reports from the state level to federal agencies. The analytical aspects of this information processing are fairly sophisticated, for they must allow the necessary interpretations of data that bear on policy considerations regarding the operation of the comprehensive guidance system in the state.

This section has outlined in a somewhat technical nonspecific manner the general informational requirements of the proposed comprehensive guidance system. Without focusing on the unique needs and information processing capability of an individual school system, it is difficult to be more specific. The comments in the following section concerning the functioning of the proposed system are more concrete than the discussion above.

HOW THE STUDENT CAREER GUIDANCE
SYSTEM MIGHT FUNCTION

This description of how the proposed system might function is presented chronologically so that the reader can follow the process easily. The description is offered at the risk of our appearing to be more sure of specific features of the system than we are. It should be regarded, then, as a highly tentative description, designed to illustrate a number of possibilities. To simplify our discussion, we refer to a junior high school and a four-year senior high, although we might just as well have chosen a three-year senior high school.

To avoid confusion, we should note that the term *school* is used both in the sense of an individual school and in the sense of a school system — such as junior and senior high schools. Other terms used in a unique manner are defined where they are first used.

Many of the components and procedures we discuss are already a reality in United States schools, although we know of no school that has implemented *all* the components of the system under discussion.

Presecondary School

Where there is an administrative need for ninth-grade course selections to be made prior to the student's entry to the ninth grade, the student career-guidance system begins no later than in the latter part of the eighth grade. At this time the students are given a basic orientation to the guidance system. This orientation, which includes an overview of the program, focuses on the benefits to the student of active and positive participation — namely, getting the most out of the next four years, completing the secondary school period with the best possible plans for the future, and obtaining the most appropriate training to follow through on the plans.

In the orientation, the steps in the process are explained and emphasis is placed on the fact that the students will be increasingly responsible for the outcomes or the lack of them. This is the first of many times that this point is made as the student is encouraged to move from being directed and dependent to being a directing, self-reliant individual in the educational process. Although this orientation may be given by the junior high school guidance staff, it probably is better for the senior high school guidance staff, with whom the students will be interacting for the next four years, to be responsible for this presentation. At the conclusion of the presentation, materials designed to reinforce the presentation for the students and to gain the parents' understanding of and support for the program are distributed.

After a reasonable interval — say, a month — the eighth-grade students as a group are again contacted. At this time a set of (yet to be developed) self-assessment instruments, to be scored or evaluated by the student, are administered. Most of the information obtained during this process is seen only by the student. The primary exception to this is the transmission from school files of certain basic data (biographic, demographic, and scholastic) about the student to the high school to provide the starting point for the aggregate student data base that is essential to the management and evaluation of the program by the school and state agencies.

This initial self-assessment yields, for the students, information created in such form as to provide them with a profile of themselves (achievements to date, plans for the future, interests, etc.) that can be compared with other students' profiles or in the profiles of hypothetical students. The information becomes the first entry in the Student Log.

The Student Log is a set of materials containing personal information which the student maintains over the next four years and which the student may consider to be completely private, never to be shared with others. At the student's discretion, other information in the Student Log may be shared with parents, teachers, or guidance staff. The third class of information in the Student Log is semipublic information, maintained by the school, probably in automated files. It includes basic biographic and demographic data, grades, test scores, and all the other information about the student that is maintained in the School File. The School File does not include medical data, sensitive faculty and administrative reports, or memoranda concerning the personal problems of the students.

The Student Log, to which the student has access at any time, contains all the information that the student has contributed or that has been accumulated as a result of her or his participation in the guidance process. The School File, on the other hand, contains the types of information normally kept about students as they progress through the educational system. As noted above, this is semipublic information to which authorized school staff or parents may have access without the approval of the student. In addition, the School File contains some information considered private, but it is maintained in such a manner that the student's identity is protected. Analyses of these data may be returned to the students for their own purposes or may be used to meet the school's need for longitudinal data about individuals in the system, but with complete anonymity for individual students.

When the students prepare their initial entries in the Student Log, the confrontation process begins. In a group, the students are led through a self-analysis process by the high school guidance staff. Sample student descriptions are used to illustrate the significant (or insignificant) elements in descriptions, and the students are shown how they can critically evaluate their self-assessment and judge whether it is adequate for their purposes. At this juncture it is likely that many, if not most, of the students conclude that their own assessment and career planning may be incomplete or unrealistic, or that it may commit them to undesirable involvements that they had not been aware of. At this point, the pertinence and usefulness of the career guidance system is discussed with them so that they can understand how, through their own efforts, they can improve their plans and acquire critical skills.

The eighth-grade students are next presented with material about the various high school programs. This set of presentations involves both the teaching staff and the guidance staff of the high school. The teaching staff provides descriptions of course prerequisites and requirements, as well as the career possibilities of the various academic programs. The guidance staff presents various strategies for program and course selection that would be appropriate for students in a variety of situations — for example, for students with no strong interests or plans, for those with tentative plans and interests, and for those with strong interests and plans. As they consider the various academic programs and specific course selections, students are urged to review the initial self-assessment materials in their Student Log.

At this stage in the process, both the high school and the junior high school guidance staff enter into an intensive counseling phase with individual students who are making their course selections. The students are encouraged to interact as much as possible with their parents, their counselors, and the teaching staff in making their initial choices of courses and programs.

A valuable aid to the choice process at this point is a prediction system developed from the school records of previous students, whereby students are informed of the statistically probable outcomes of their choices, both in terms of high school curriculum and post-high school involvements. Included in the predictions are the pathways students are likely to follow, given certain initial choices, the expected performance levels, and the past performance and personal characteristics of the student in question. (It is necessary and is also an excellent instructional opportunity to make sure at this point that students understand the probabilistic nature of predictions.)

Early Secondary School

In this phase of the process the effective integration of the teaching and guidance functions becomes critical to the success of the concept. The initial stages of the various curriculums are designed so that their elements (courses, groups of courses, and the academic and vocational skills taught) are, to the greatest extent possible, transferable from one curriculum or educational pathway to another, with a minimum loss of time for students who switch from one to another curriculum. As a part of instruction in the initial stages of the curriculums, materials are presented that allow the students to see how the course of study is applicable to a class, or classes, or careers, as well as what cognitive and psychomotor skills are required in classes of careers.

The objective is to give the students the broadest possible exposure to, and the greatest flexibility to explore, the academic fields and possible careers. Throughout this early secondary period, teachers, guidance staff, and parents consciously encourage exploration and experimentation on the part of the students. The dangers of premature commitment to a particular educational pathway and also the critical importance of obtaining competence in fundamental skills are repeatedly emphasized.

In addition to the presentation of traditional instructional programs to students, this period includes some new curricular elements, namely, formal course work in acquiring a general base of knowledge about classes of occupations and careers. Such course work also includes instruction regarding strategies and resources to be utilized as the student desires, as well as the need for additional career and occupational planning. Information about local, state, regional, and national career opportunities and trends is necessary so that the students can begin to test their initial career conceptions and plans against the real world.

Critical to the career guidance system is the acquisition of decision-making skills. Our tentative belief is that the development of these skills is best taught in the context of career guidance. Assuming this to be the case, a course or courses in this area, taught by specially trained instructors, becomes a part of the early secondary school curriculum.

Also during this early period, the school's administrative, teaching, and guidance staffs work together to facilitate the process of occupational sampling by the students. Such a program is encouraged by having managerial, technical, and professional people visit the schools to provide some introduction to a variety of careers. This type of presentation might be made within the instructional program itself. For instance, an engineer, a designer, or an architect could be invited to present certain instructional materials in basic algebra or geometry. Here again, the goal is to integrate traditional instruction with steps to facilitate career development. Additional efforts in this area include instructive field visits, work exploration, internships, and job simulations.

During the early secondary school period, there is a continuous monitoring of the guidance process with feedback to the students and the school staff. At a minimum, this monitoring and its feedback occur on a semester cycle, though much of the student-produced information is generated on a continuing basis. Students are encouraged to record impressions, opinions, and possible revisions in their self-perceptions and career plans (or their career perceptions, if they have no plans) as they have ideas and gain information relevant to their developing careers.

At the conclusion of the semester, the guidance staff reviews the completed course work with the students. The students are encouraged to review their Logs, and to use their newly acquired information and the self-assessments that they made during the semester, as they make decisions about their future academic programs. Although most of the information developed by the students in this process is retained by them in their individual Student Logs, certain summary information such as end of course evaluations is transmitted to the School File for use in individual analyses (for return to the students) and in general evaluations of the system itself.

Normally, individual counseling with the guidance staff takes place during the feedback and review periods only when the student desires it. The guidance staff contacts the students only when the School File indicates that a student is not participating. Depending upon the desires of the school and the local community, the student is strongly urged to participate in the program, but may be excused from it. In other words, participation in the career guidance program may, in some schools, be entirely voluntary. It is still necessary, however, for students to provide the school with a minimum amount of data for planning purposes.

By the last part of the early secondary school period, the students have gone through several semester cycles, during which most of them have explored several areas of interest. At this time they again go through a structured process to evaluate the status of their current career planning and to make curriculum choices that will, in most cases, represent firm commitments during the remainder of the secondary school period. Through group instruction, the students are aided in evaluating their Student Logs. They are also given the available information from the School File, analyzed and presented in a manner to encourage a positive confrontation between their expressed plans, strategies, and desires and their performance and accomplishments to date. The outcome of this confrontation is a reinforcement of their existing plans (or strategies for developing plans) or a reformulation of them.

Late Secondary School

During this stage the breadth of exploration narrows rapidly for most students. The career planning that most students have engaged in just prior to this stage undergoes only minor modifications if their efforts to date have been effective. Many, if not most, students will have made basic decisions about their futures — whether to interrupt studies prior to graduation, have no further education beyond high school, go to college immediately following high school, or have a period of work and then more education.

The semester cycle of formal reviews of completed courses and work-related experiences and their implications for the students' career planning continues during the early part of the late secondary school stage. But again, for most students, the thrust of the effort is generally toward a refinement of plans, not radical changes — for example, making preliminary plans to pursue a career in engineering rather than science, as contrasted with deciding to change from a career as a lawyer to one as a steelworker. We would not discourage drastic changes, however, for it is better that they be made at this point than later.

At this stage increased emphasis on occupational sampling seems quite appropriate. The administrative, teaching, and guidance staffs, working with employers in the community, can go far toward providing students with a good opportunity to test their tentative career plans. Curriculums are designed so that students in the junior and senior years of high school have sufficient time to participate in actual occupational settings. Such opportunities are carefully worked out between the school and the employer so that the student has an opportunity to observe and participate in a valid sample of occupational activities, and so that the employer is willing to provide structured and meaningful feedback to the student and the school.

In the senior year the student participates in a comprehensive attainment program. The program is designed primarily to provide assessment data to the students that will assist them in testing their self-perceptions and career plans and in making their decisions for the immediate post-high school period. A secondary purpose of this effort is to give the school information about the students so that it can evaluate the effectiveness of the career guidance program and identify areas for possible improvement.

Working with the information described above and their Student Logs, the students can decide upon the choices open to them for employment or continuing education. During this period of decision making, the guidance staff, in cooperation with the teaching staff, is available to work with students who feel a need for counseling. The involvement of the teaching staff at this time is stressed. Because teachers have had the opportunity over the four-year period to observe and work with the students more closely than have other staff members in the school, their informal insights and appraisals, given to the student in a supportive manner, prove useful to the students in their decision making.

After students have made their decisions, the guidance staff provides direct individualized assistance to them in both job and college placement. In this activity the guidance staff is not acting as a decision maker for the students, but rather as an information resource with experience, contacts, and expertise to help students implement the decisions they have made.

As the final step in the secondary school stage of the student career guidance process, the students participate in an exit survey. The survey is designed to disclose the depth and appropriateness of their planning as well as the extent to which they have made, and are acting on, decisions consistent with their planning. This is the only step in the process where the primary purpose of the information is to serve the needs of the school instead of the student. This end-of-process measure is comparable with the beginning-of-process measure that the students provided in the eighth grade. This information is essential to the management and evaluation of the system at the school level and also provides aggregate information to intermediate and state agencies.

Postsecondary School

A postgraduation step in the process is to obtain information from the students a year or more after they have left high school. Such feedback is essential to answer key questions about the adequacy of the student career guidance system. Did the program aid the students in making post-high school career decisions that, in the light of their experience to date, were good ones? Were they better than they would have been without such a program?

A secondary purpose of the follow-up is to satisfy whatever interest recent graduates may have in relating their own activities to those of their classmates. Respondents in the follow-up study receive a copy of the aggregate information about their class—how many classmates are doing what, or whether or not their current status is consistent with their plans at the time they left high school.

As mentioned earlier, we know of no system that functions entirely as the proposed system does, for the simple reason that implementing such a system poses many problems yet to be solved. These problems are discussed in the next chapter, along with some steps that might be taken toward their solution.

CHAPTER 5

Some Impressions, Problems, and Ideas for Implementation

The preceding chapters focused on concepts and on ideal or optimal situations. Principles and processes were described and elaborated upon without the constraints of practical considerations. The authors recognize, however, that the realities of the current educational scene must be confronted if the proposed system is to be fully implemented. Accordingly, we now turn to a number of factors in the educational environment that must be considered, problems that will require solutions, and initial ideas for implementing the concepts discussed earlier. In the absence of systematic surveys, we can only offer impressions. We leave it to the reader to decide whether these impressions have sufficient validity to justify the tentative conclusions reached.

The first and most relevant impression is that while we have proposed a broadening and intensification of the career guidance function, many recent events raise serious questions about the future of career guidance. The following observations illustrate this impression:

- The Office of Education has eliminated almost all mention of guidance in its administrative structure.
- Guidance consultants in state departments of education appear to be less effectual than in the past.
- Categorical aid for guidance, such as that of the days of National Defense Education Act, has almost totally disappeared.

- Researchers in guidance and career development continue to have great difficulty in obtaining financial support.
- Companies such as Science Research Associates, Guidance Associates, and others have shifted their attention away from the production of guidance materials toward the development of curriculum materials in more financially remunerative areas.
- Significant numbers of counselors in places like Chicago have been returned to the classroom.
- Faced with rapidly rising costs, many schools are eliminating the very career guidance services recommended in the previous chapters.

On the other hand, there are some more optimistic signs:

- The American Vocational Association Vocational Guidance Division has been growing steadily in membership.
- During the spring of 1975 the American Personnel Guidance Association was successful in developing a congressional bill for new support of guidance which eventually will be incorporated under the vocational amendments.
- USOE's Office of Career Education has, since 1975, funded a number of guidance projects.
- The Ohio State Center for Vocational Education and American Institutes for Research have experienced much demand for their products.
- The National Advisory Council on Career Education has designed a broad-range program of federal legislation including guidance components.

We conclude that the future of career guidance is, at best, uncertain. It has gained support from the career education movement, but career education still has far to go to become a full-blown reality, despite the innovations which it has spawned in our high schools. Furthermore, counselors do not seem to be fully involved in the movement, and the integration of career education into the curriculum is far from "wall-to-wall." Work experience programs are growing in number, but still do not involve large numbers of students. Comprehensive high schools are still inadequate in providing placement services for students who do not continue their education after high school. Follow-up studies are seldom conducted. In short, there is much to be done.

There are, however, signs of progress. Most high schools today boast legitimate career resource centers, whereas five years ago the most common signs of career guidance were in nooks and on bulletin boards. Although the quality of these career centers may vary, they have some common characteristics.

Probably the best thing about these ubiquitous career centers is that they are there. They present visible evidence to students and parents that the school cares enough about the career development of its students to allocate some space and money toward the cause. And, because the career centers are there, they are used.

The materials typically are well organized, easily obtainable, and kept current. The centers are often tended by paraprofessionals. The skill and attitude of attendants has much to do with student usage. Some students come to the center of their own volition, but most are directed there by counselors or teachers. The better centers have lots of giveaway materials and provide means by which visitors may reproduce and take home relevant information. These career centers often relieve counselors of other career guidance responsibilities, such as coordinating arrangements for guest speakers, field trips, etc.

On the other hand, since they are frequently not located near the counseling area, they tend to be overlooked. Some counselors regard career centers as something apart from their area of work. An even greater problem is that the presence of a career center causes some counselors unconsciously to abrogate their career counseling responsibilities by shunting students to the centers and then dismissing the students from their minds.

The heralded career guidance curricular infusions do not seem to be much in evidence. The business and industrial arts departments are still the bastions of vocational guidance. Some schools, particularly those with flexible programing, have introduced career exploration courses. These are largely optional and not highly popular. The traditional "vocational units" were eliminated from social studies curriculums during the post-Sputnik purges and have not returned. Few departments are willing to give up enough time for the unit approach, and infusion only occurs with dedicated, imaginative leadership. Furthermore, high school teachers, with their allegiances to their various disciplines, are much less amenable to the introduction of "outside" matter into their instruction than are their more ecumenical colleagues at the intermediate and elementary levels.

Available assessment tools are still used only occasionally in career guidance at the high school level. Many counselors remain untutored in the proper use of tests. To many of them, all standardized assessment is suspect. Group "intelligence tests" are anathema. Aptitude tests are also scorned by the champions of the disadvantaged. Even achievement tests are losing favor in the rush to criterion-referenced tests as "the answer." Use of vocational interest tests does not seem to have markedly increased in response to the career education movement. The Kuder and the Strong-Campbell tests are still available and still used in the same old ways—that is, with limited effect. The Differential Aptitude Test remains a perennial favorite. Interpretation of test results in terms of their implications for career development varies from adequate to poor.

Old customs die hard. The traditional career days and nights, despite their well-known shortcomings, remain a part of the high school scene. At worst, they are good public relations gestures. At best, they provide mass exposure to a few occupations for some interested students.

Work experience and career exploration opportunities have been introduced or expanded in many high schools as a direct result of the career education movement. Only a minority of students take advantage of these opportunities but the number is increasing. It is no small task to establish and supervise a good work experience program, and some schools have not been able to afford it. Another barrier is the natural conservatism of most students. Many are afraid to venture forth from the security of the school environment. Even for the willing students, there are barriers: parental objections, transportation, incompatibility with other commitments, not enough time, etc. Like so many other noble concepts, work experience encounters rough going in practice. On the other hand, cooperative education is expanding rapidly across the country.

Most guidance programs are fragmented and lack any systematic approach to information gathering and reporting. It is difficult to predict the probability of adoption by school districts of a comprehensive guidance system, based primarily on a well-developed management information system, providing feedback to students, the school, and the state. The probability of adoption could be increased if the school administrative staff and the school board could be convinced of its worth and persuaded to provide financial support. The need is to keep costs to somewhere between $1 and $1.25 per student. Since instruction consumes approximately 80 percent of the budget in many schools, leaving relatively little for operational expenses, it is unrealistic to think of per pupil expenditures for career guidance that go much beyond the $1.00–$1.50 range.

Almost anyone knowledgeable in the field of guidance will, we believe, agree on the need for a comprehensive guidance system, utilizing a systematic and well-developed information system. As we have found in the past, however, demand is not always commensurate with need. Because of the budgetary limitations of most school districts, the question is not can this item be added to the budget, but rather, does it have sufficient priority to reduce or supplant other budget items? Whether career guidance has such priority is questionable.

PROBLEMS

The problems identified here are not to be considered comprehensive. They come from informal sources and are intended to convey some of the more important or pervasive problematic aspects that need consideration and resolution. These observations have been grouped as follows: General, Financial, School, Staff, and Student.

General

Good assessment, the key to the Confrontation/Reformulation Model, presents several problems. There is strong resistance in some powerful quarters to testing in the cognitive domain. The limitations of assessment in the noncognitive domain are well known. Developing measures for this assessment will be a challenge for some performance objectives. Many of the most desirable outcomes of career guidance are difficult, at best, to measure. For decision-making skill, for example, there is no universally accepted measure of competency. Whether the decision-making measure recently developed as part of the College Board's Career Skills Assessment Program will fill the bill remains to be seen. Thus, it appears that legalistic prohibitions and psychometric limitations may hamper the implementation of the system despite many promising efforts.

Another problem area concerns the confidentiality of individual data. With the proposed system, it seems that this issue can be met satisfactorily, but legislative action that goes beyond the Buckley amendment could present additional problems. It is also possible that problems could arise from political constraints which could emerge and become significant if a program such as this one began to have a real impact. (There is some experience to date with the political issues and their impact on such straightforward systems as testing programs.) The potential impact of a guidance system such as that proposed could be much greater when one considers its utilization of such information as employment trends and its possible influence on the composition of the work force. Such considerations could bring powerful vested interests to bear on the system.

Financial

Probably the most pervasive and most severe problems will be encountered in the financial area. At present the vast majority of school districts measure their per pupil expenditures for guidance in terms of dollars or the very low tens of dollars. It is unlikely, within the next five or even ten years, that many school districts will be able to increase appreciably their funding for guidance services. Accordingly, it seems appropriate that any effort to provide a substantially improved guidance system must assume only small increases in funds available for implementing the system at the school district level. This is a very serious constraint.

If we were to add $100 per student to a school district's annual capital expenditures, we are sure we could address the career guidance problem. How much can be done for an additional $1 or $2 per student? And even the addition of this amount may not be a realistic expectation. Guidance departments in every school district must compete with instructional areas, school administration, extracurricular activities, and building maintenance for the education dollar. Guidance in many school districts is regarded as a budget luxury, rather than as serving the legitimate needs of students. Thus, a major need in guidance is increased productivity or "throughput," that is, more students need to receive more and better service through the application of the same level of staff and resources. How to achieve this is an unsolved problem.

School

A great deal has been said about the importance of the high school as an exploratory experience prior to entry into the world of work. In actual practice, however, it has been difficult to break the lockstep pattern wherein the requirements imposed by college preparation and courses mandated by state legislatures leave few opportunities for exploration. As districts have found themselves in a financial bind, some have reduced the length of the school day, restricting even further the possibilities for exploration through elective courses or work experience. It is quite possible that this has had the effect of too early commitment by many students and no commitment by others.

The problem of valid occupational sampling by the student is a real one. Not only is there the serious question of whether the tasks performed by adolescents represent a valid sampling of any occupation, but also there is the real problem of sampling a range of occupations, particularly in areas dominated by a single or few industries. Under such circumstances, the school has to stress approaches which increase awareness of other options available in areas beyond the region served by the school. This is necessary, not only to serve the needs of a mobile population, but to prevent the school from being used to satisfy the needs of special interests rather than to widen opportunities for the student in the world of work.

Staff

Because of the continuing shortage of well-trained personnel, new programs must be self-explanatory, require minimum expertise, involve the least possible administrative attention, and lend themselves to implementation via group activities that can be led by the combined efforts of teachers, counselors, and paraprofessionals. Further, not many school staff members have the training necessary to properly utilize the feedback we propose to provide them with, particularly the results of an expanded test program, probably including new, unfamiliar instruments requiring cautious interpretation. Most contemporary teachers and counselors are simply unprepared to offer the full range of services that we propose.

Students

In assuming that students will plan and act in rational ways when properly guided and provided with the necessary materials, instruction, and incentives, we may fail to recognize individual differences in style and in ability to confront problems. Many students may be incapable of the highly rational approach to career planning that most well-planned systems, including the one proposed, require. Perhaps such a systematic approach is a desired goal; whether more than a minority of the students are capable of pursuing it remains to be seen.

Consider, for example, the proposed comprehensive exit testing. Unless students recognize the crucial relationship between this testing and their individual career planning, we question its chances of success. We also see serious unsolved problems in motivating all students to take the Student Log seriously. Again, they will have to be convinced of the important relationship between their personal record keeping and their planning for the future.

We are also concerned about the unforeseen long-term effects of all school interventions, including those proposed in these pages. What, for example, will be the cumulative impact of comprehensive senior-year attainment assessment? Will it discourage innovative teaching? If a larger share of school resources is devoted to career guidance, what other aspects of the school will suffer? Our fear is that school resource allocation tends to be a zero-sum game: gains in one area tend to result in losses in other areas. (A research effort to monitor long-term effects is proposed in Chapter 6.)

Finally, as useful background for implementation, we point to three past efforts at ETS of which we are repeatedly reminded as we think about the proposed system. These were Systems for Assessment and Guidance in Education (SAGE), Educational Systems Information Program (ESIP), and Educational Guidance Information System (EGIS). Despite their intrinsic virtue, they met rejection in the cold light of day for at least three reasons: (1) They were too costly; (2) they violated the "let me do it for myself, mother" verity; and (3) they failed to resolve the eternal conflict of different information needs at different educational levels. What is proposed here may contain some of the same kernels of its own demise.

IDEAS FOR IMPLEMENTATION

Assuming that the impressions and problems summarized above reflect, with at least a modicum of accuracy, the realities of guidance practices in contemporary high schools in the United States and the reasons for the limited success of past efforts along these lines, what conclusions can we draw about implementing the proposed system?

First, its cost will be the major barrier to its implementation. Second, gaining acceptance of a comprehensive system with many unsolved problems will be a major hurdle. Even if the concepts inherent in the proposed system are accepted as sound, translating them into practice is quite another matter. These conclusions have a number of implications for school systems interested in implementing the proposed system.

As far as cost is concerned, the obvious recommendation is that every possible step be taken to keep the cost of implementing the system to minimal levels. But, however valid, this is not a very helpful recommendation. The fact is that, by and large, we have proposed additional educational services, not alternatives to present services. We have said that implementing new career guidance services must in no way diminish the quality of the traditional instructional program. What we propose must augment and strengthen the educational process, not supplant any part of it. Thus, the inevitable consequence will be increased costs. And, even if a concentrated effort is made to keep the per pupil cost of the proposed components minimal, the increased cost of implementing the total system is certain to be substantial.

The only route to implementing the kind of system proposed is the stepwise modular route. Specifically, we recommend the following procedures for organizations and government agencies involved in developing career guidance systems and in gaining their acceptance in the schools:

1. Design each component of the total system so that it can both stand alone and be compatible with other components of the system. The installation of any one component should not require that other components be in place. When other components are added to the system, the overlap with existing components should be minimal.

2. Design components in such a way that they can "piggyback" on existing guidance procedures and materials rather than duplicate elements already in use. (The "planned obsolescence" attributed to the auto industry must never be the practice.) For the same reason, components should be modifiable and adaptable to unique local situations.

3. Design components to be compatible with the products and services provided by all the major test publishers and service organizations, for the reasons cited above.

4. Give priority to components that will not require extensive in-service training for their proper use.

5. Where possible, design and disseminate components and services so that they will be viewed as integral parts of the school's educational program, rather than as ancillary components and services ("frills"), which are subject to the vagaries of the school budget.

6. Assist schools through an extensive advisory service that would:

   a. Identify ways of reducing internal expenses, for example, through the use of group guidance procedures or by making use of career guidance materials which are available at little cost. So much of value has already been done in career guidance and is in the public domain that developers of guidance materials would be foolish not to build upon that which is germane to their efforts. Many directors of exemplary career education programs readily attribute their ideas and materials to other sources. Their originality was in assembling them in a unique fashion.

   b. Provide advice on ways of obtaining federal or state support for their guidance program, workshops, or local research and development efforts.

   c. Provide technical advice on using local resources to develop materials and components.

   d. Suggest priorities for gradually building a comprehensive career guidance system.

   e. Provide well-documented evidence on the cost effectiveness of alternative components — evidence which school administrators can use to strengthen their case in obtaining local financial support for their programs. Where such evidence is not available, schools should be assisted in developing realistic cost estimates on the basis of local conditions.

   f. Assist guidance departments in taking steps to demonstrate the impact of their efforts on the growth of individual students. Only in this way can guidance functions compete for funding with other school functions, the results of which are usually more visible to the public.

   g. Provide advice on how to obtain local support for projected plans, including how to conduct needs assessments, how to establish objectives, and how to assemble their own programs in collaboration with parents, community leaders, and employers.

In general, then, developers of new services and materials should strongly resist the tendency to prepare huge prepackaged programs. Many people are resistant, if not hostile, to large, comprehensive programs. Many would rather do it themselves (although few follow through), and few indicate that such systems have high priority in times of shrinking budgets. Moreover, the authors' experience has shown that even where complex data reporting systems were implemented, few schools had the expertise to take advantage of the data provided. In fact, we know of some institutions that abandoned programs because they were embarrassed by the deluge of data that they felt incapable of using. We therefore caution against the development of a highly complex system resulting in data overload, and we urge the development of local capabilities, thereby lessening dependence upon outside sources for continuation of the program.

It should not be forgotten that different educational settings present different problems that call for different solutions. Rural schools, for example, have some handicaps in implementing comprehensive career guidance which need special attention. A particular problem is the lack of a range of accessible work experience opportunities. Rural high school students simply cannot explore many careers. Yet, increasingly, jobs on the farms and in the forests are being mechanized, and young people must move to the cities to seek careers in fields which they have no opportunities to explore. A feasible, wide-reaching work exploratory program for rural youth would be a real boon.

In addition, we offer the following random observations:

1. Testing the components of the proposed system is done best in local, pilot situations, rather than in a full-blown state program. Under the more controllable conditions of a local school system ideas that prove unworkable can be abandoned and good components can be expanded to other sites.
2. If the first school systems to adopt components of a guidance system are well known and respected, the probability that other systems will adopt the components is increased.
3. A certain amount of reinvention of the wheel will be necessary. Inevitably, this means starting with a needs assessment. The process is more important than the results. Enhancing the current curriculum should be emphasized.
4. Follow-up studies are obviously important, but they present difficulties for many high schools. To be done properly they

require time and money. However, the most important element, which is usually missing, is direction. This is why
most high schools fail to complete follow-ups. The answer
lies in adequate back-up. A local graduate school of education can usually provide it at a modest fee. This resource
could be recommended to local schools.

5. Organizations like American Institutes for Research, National Institute of Education, the Ohio State Center for Vocational Education, the ERIC Clearinghouse for Career Education, the American Personnel and Guidance Association,
the National Vocational Guidance Association, the American
School Counselor Association, and the National Association
of Pupil Personnel Administration have common interests
in career guidance. It makes more sense to proceed in collaboration than to proceed unilaterally. A cooperative approach would appeal to many potential participants.

6. Before a prolonged experiment or developmental program
is undertaken in a particular area it is essential to obtain an
assessment of the demand for the resulting product or service by potential clients. Otherwise, a well-conceived program may join the graveyard of other programs of the past
for which there was a theoretical need but little demand
from the schools.

7. If a career guidance program is to have any chance of success, it must have the enthusiastic support of the school's
staff (teachers, counselors, administrators). Before a model
such as that proposed here can be implemented, the staff
will need to be introduced to the philosophy underlying
career guidance, its general aims and objectives, and the
basic principles of career development. If the staff becomes
aware of the aims and objectives of the career guidance program and are given an active role in developing the program,
they are more likely to become enthusiastic supporters of
the concept.

    The staff should be involved in all phases of program
development, from planning through evaluation, including
the development of objectives from the needs assessment,
the development of job placement services and occupational
information, and the determination of what program assessment data should be collected and how those data will be
used to modify program objectives.

8. It is inevitable and proper for each district to define its own set of goals, objectives, and activities. Some schools may offer courses or activities in occupational information and concentrate more on work experience. Some schools may attempt to integrate career guidance units into the classroom, whereas other schools may seek some other method for delivering career guidance activities. Some may emphasize instruction in decision making, others may focus on self-awareness. Some may try to do all these things and many more. In general, no single set of aims is sufficient for the needs of all guidance departments and communities.

Needs assessment can be a valuable tool in determining career guidance program goals. Parents, teachers, students, and counselors all can contribute to the assessment. A possible first step in implementing a comprehensive needs assessment is to have a group of parents, teachers, students, and counselors develop a list of goals for career guidance, and then have all concerned, including students, rank order the desirability of each goal.

Students can, and indeed should, contribute to the determination of program goals. Few programs have much chance of success if they are aimed at areas that students regard as irrelevant or uninteresting. If a student does not see a need to gain better study habits for himself, a program designed to improve his study habits will likely fail.

After identifying major program goals, each goal should be broken down into specific performance objectives. For example, the goal, "every student will have a knowledge of his interests, abilities, and other characteristics," might be broken down to a sequence of objectives, the accomplishment of which implies the achievement of the goal. Such performance objectives might be the following:

1. The students will be able to distinguish among abilities, interests, values, physical traits, and personal-social behaviors.
2. The students will be able to identify three major sources of information about each of the characteristics and their standing on these sources of information.
3. The student will summarize, in a log, information about himself on each of the characteristic areas.
4. The student will be able, to the satisfaction of a counselor,

to discuss this assessment information and relate that information to his future plans.

Once the purposes, goals, and objectives of a career guidance program are specified and materials collected or developed for the accomplishment of the goals, students, teachers, and counselors must have an ample opportunity to field-test the program. The field-test might be limited to one or two pilot studies in the district. The key to moving from the previous stages to an implementation stage is to emphasize a gradual change to the newly designed program. During the field-testing phase, which should encompass the first year of the program, specific weaknesses in the program should be identified. In particular, instances of professional undertraining of teachers and counselors should be noted and steps to remedy the difficulties should be undertaken. Significant revisions or replacement of material that does not meet the criteria for success will likely occur. Additional inservice or preservice activities for teachers may be needed to improve implementation or competencies.

Earlier we mentioned that the proposed system has "many unsolved problems." The solution of these problems is critical to gaining acceptance of the proposed system. In the following chapter, we outline a broad program of research and development which focuses on these problems.

CHAPTER **6**

National Priorities
for Research and Development

In thinking about an ideal high school career guidance system we repeatedly encountered unanswered questions — about career development, educational effects, optimal guidance procedures, to name a few. We had to make assumptions about the answers, frequently with no real confidence that the assumptions were tenable. We also referred to certain instruments and procedures as if they were available when, in fact, they are not — at least not in the exact form that is required. In this chapter, 12 needed research studies and 17 needed components and services are briefly described and are evaluated by the authors with respect to five factors. We then offer a few comments about how to decide on priorities for research, components, and services.

In this kind of planning, one immediately encounters the issue of research vs. development. Throughout the preceding chapters, the need for more fundamental knowledge of the nature of student development and decision making has been mentioned. If the immediate needs of the schools were no consideration, we would call for a national halt on developmental activities and recommend a focus of all available funds[5] on gaining a greater understanding of the psychological and sociological processes which underlie the development

---

5. "Available funds" refers here to the funds that any government agency, foundation, or educational institution may have earmarked for research and development in the general area of career guidance.

of careers, and a truer picture of the current state and needs of career guidance in this country.

But the immediate needs of the schools *are* a consideration. We do not need a large-scale survey to know that all is not well with our schools. The illnesses described in the Introduction are real. One has only to read current newspapers to see that a large proportion of our schools are faced with financial crises. Guidance services are under fire and are being cut back, even eliminated, in some schools. To justify current expenditures — to say nothing of justifying increased expenditures — efforts to increase the effectiveness of career guidance services must be continued. We must proceed with developmental activities on the basis of available research, and *at the same time* take steps to enlarge that base of fundamental knowledge on which such work depends.

The question, then, is not one of either/or, but of how much of each kind of activity. What proportion of available funds should be invested in research, and what proportion in product or service development? (For these purposes, "research" is defined broadly to include both basic and applied investigations or, in general, any knowledge-seeking that is not designed to produce a specific service or product.) It is tempting to recommend that the split be fifty-fifty, but such a split is difficult to defend except on the grounds of symmetry. A better rule might be to designate a lower limit for research — to guarantee that a minimal amount of research continues — and let additional research expenditures depend on operational needs. In other words, if, in developing a specific product or service, the need arises for certain data or knowledge, research expenditures in addition to the designated minimum would be budgeted.

In accordance with this strategy, we would recommend that 20 percent of available funds be allocated for general research in the area of career development and decision making. Special purpose studies, for example, a literature search or a validity study, designed to answer an immediate question or solve a current problem, would be supported from appropriations or grants in addition to the 20 percent.

In the following pages, 29 required studies and developmental projects are described and rated in accordance with five factors that are summarized in Table 1. Since it is difficult to compare the urgency of a specific research study with the urgency of a developmental project, the research studies and the developmental projects are grouped in two separate sections.

Table 1. FACTORS FOR ESTABLISHING PRIORITIES

Factors	High (3)	Medium (2)	Low (1)
1. State of the art – degree to which method or technology exists to do research or to develop a particular component	Method fully available	Moderately available; some methodological work necessary or problems to be solved	Much methodological or theory development necessary
2. Criticalness – as element of proposed system	System cannot function without it	System could function but not well	System could function without it
3. Cost – to conduct study, or to develop component to a degree suitable for field testing in one or more schools	More than $250,000	$100,000 to $250,000	Less than $100,000
4. Need – extent to which relevant research results are now available or component is available from testing, publishing, or service organizations, or is in place in the schools	Nothing, or very little available	Available but only partially adequate or too expensive or not well known	At least moderately adequate component available which is widely utilized
5. Speed to completion – how soon the product, service, or study might be ready for field-testing or dissemination	Very soon within 1 year	More than 1 year but less than 3	More than 3 years

Although the factors are self-explanatory, the assumptions made in selecting two of them should be made explicit. First, we assume that, in order to generate useful research results and components as quickly as possible, priority should be given to research and development for which the methodology now exists. Nevertheless, we hope that readers will note the areas needing methodological advances and that some readers will be motivated to design relevant research efforts. Second, we assume that priority should be given to research and development that costs the least, or even better, is the most cost beneficial. Thus, cost should be evaluated in relation to the value of probable outcomes. For the research studies, the cost rating is based on a rough estimate of the cost of conducting the full-scale study.

Deciding what constituted a separate study or project was a difficult task. In general, we followed the structure of the earlier chapters, and discussed the studies or components as they are described there. We departed from these descriptions only where we knew that one way or several alternative ways of satisfying a particular need already existed. In such a case our recommendation is that first the existing components be identified and evaluated.

As parts of a comprehensive system, certain components ideally should be developed in conjunction with other components. The list of studies and projects as a whole should not, then, be regarded as a menu from which selections can be made without regard for the relationships that may exist among them.

Following the descriptions of each possible study or product, evaluative comments are offered. These comments represent the consensus of the Career Guidance Design team, and are summarized at the end of this chapter.

RESEARCH STUDIES REQUIRED

1. National Longitudinal Surveys of Student Development

In previous chapters we have repeatedly cited questions or untested assumptions that need further research. The following are examples:

- What are the major determinants of the particular career decisions that students make, including decisions to take particular courses of instruction, to select academic or vocational programs, to interrupt or terminate their formal education, and to pursue certain posthigh school pathways?

- To what extent have students interrupted or terminated their high school education primarily for financial reasons, and to what extent has this resulted from ignorance of available financial data?
- To what extent do the guidance needs of high-school-age girls differ from those of boys? Can we assume that the psychodynamics of career development of girls and boys are the same?
- By what processes and experiences do young people obtain self-insight?
- By what processes and experiences do young people acquire values, interests, and occupational preferences?
- Do students who have opportunities to gain career awareness and decision-making skills in secondary school fare better after leaving secondary school than students who did not have such opportunities?
- To what extent are the posthigh school educational and vocational needs of contemporary students consistent with the learning opportunities they have in high school?[6]

Translating these types of questions into researchable hypotheses is in most cases an exceptionally difficult task, to say nothing of the task of designing manageable tests of the hypotheses. But to undertake the development of ways of facilitating career development without answers to such questions as these could result in seriously misdirected and unproductive investment of developmental funds.

This is not to say that the questions above have not already received attention. Indeed, a large bibliography of relevant research studies can readily be assembled. There are shortcomings to this research, however. Much of it was conducted 20 to 30 years ago, and there is reason to believe that contemporary influences on career development and educational outcomes may be substantially different from the past. One can hypothesize, for example, that peer-group influences on career decisions are now stronger than in the past.

6. The overlap of this list of questions and a list identified independently by Mitchell, Jones, and Krumboltz (1966) is impressive.

Past research typically has not been comprehensive, that is, it has focused on particular influences (such as counselors, parents, employment opportunities) rather than on the relative strength of various influences.

Past studies have usually focused on small samples with unique characteristics as opposed to large national samples. Moreover, the few large-sample longitudinal studies that have been conducted have resulted in the creation of large data bases and many volumes of descriptive results but only in a relatively small number of hypothesis-testing studies that might have contributed to a theory of student development.

The basic cause of this state of affairs is economic. Conducting national longitudinal studies is vastly more expensive than other research efforts; creating the data bases tends to consume all available funds. Examples of such studies are ETS's Study of Academic Growth and Prediction (described in Hilton, Beaton, and Bowers, 1971), Project TALENT (described in Flanagan et al., 1962), and The Base Year Survey of the National Longitudinal Study of the High School Class of 1972 (Hilton and Rhett, 1973). Project TALENT and the ETS Growth Study would be candidates if the interest is in long-term follow-up. If the purpose is to examine the development of a more recent cohort of students, then the NLS file is the obvious first choice. The NLS data file is well suited for the investigation of several, but clearly not all, of the questions listed. Recently a number of researchers have been funded by various federal agencies to conduct analyses of the NLS data file, and several of these studies appear to be relevant to the proposed questions. Peng and his associates (1977) have summarized these studies. A research study that focused directly on questions such as these and at the same time gleaned findings from other analyses underway would be highly appropriate.

COMMENTS

In light of the five factors cited earlier, we would say that the state of the art is fully appropriate for intensive analyses of national data files. Recent methodological developments, especially structural analysis (Jöreskog, 1970), provide powerful analytic tools heretofore unavailable.

As far as criticalness is concerned, the kind of guidance system we have proposed could function without longitudinal research, but it would be functioning on the basis of assumptions about student development that need much additional scrutiny. The cost would be

low since the required data have already been collected and processed. The need is moderate in view of the number of analyses of
the NLS file that are underway at this writing (Peng et al., 1977).
Lastly, the speed to completion is high, since the data tapes are
readily available.

2. Longitudinal Case Studies

There are limitations to the data files described here. In the NLS,
for example, the subjects were first studied as high school seniors;
the relevant questionnaire items are retrospective (for example,
"How much did your high school counselor influence your post-
high school plans?"). Although the data are probably better than
any other available, such retrospective judgments by individuals are
suspect at best. Accordingly, we strongly recommend that analyses
of existing data files be supplemented with specially designed studies, such as longitudinal case studies of small samples of contemporary students in a small sample of high schools in the United
States. Thus, the case studies would be of both schools and the students therein.

Specifically, we propose that a random sample of 10 schools be
drawn from a stratified frame of public schools and then that 10
students be randomly drawn from each school. These schools and
their students would be intensively studied for at least the next
seven years. A possible design is shown in Figure 8. In the first year
of the study, 50 students would be drawn from grade seven, and 10
each from grades eight through twelve. Thus, the sample in any one
school would consist of five seventh-graders, one eighth-grader, one
ninth-grader, and so on. At least two subjects at each grade level
(for instance, a male and a female) would be better; cost is the limit-
ing factor. This sample would provide immediate cross-sectional results spanning the secondary school years. Thereafter, each of the
students would be followed until the end of the first year following
high school graduation or, in the case of nongraduates, the year they
would have graduated. How much effort to devote to reducing sample attrition would depend on available funds. It would be highly
desirable to reduce attrition close to zero by following the subjects
wherever they might move in the United States, in school and out
of school.

Following the model of R. W. White's Lives in Progress (1952),
the intensive study of each student would include structured inter-

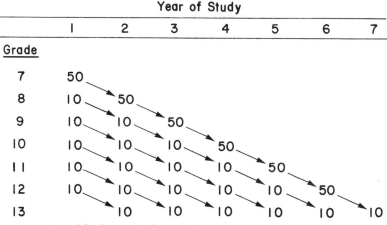

Figure 8.   Possible design for longitudinal case studies

views at least two times a year (preferably more often), administration of standardized instruments to supplement data from school files, and collection of extensive data about the schools in which the students are enrolled and the communities in which they live.

Despite the well-known shortcomings of case studies, particularly the participant-observer problem and the problem of generalizing from small samples, it is our conviction that the in-depth insights obtained would be invaluable in learning about student development, particularly about the complex interactions between student, school, and community. Such insights would also supplement and help interpret the results reported from large-scale national surveys — results which inevitably are based on less than complete data on individual students. Generalizations based on nomothetic (large-scale) studies are of little value if they have no explanatory value or validity when individual students are studied in depth. Thus, interpreting the data would involve an interplay between nomothetic and ideographic data, with the findings from each data set being tested against the other.

COMMENTS

The art of conducting case studies (that is, the state of the art) is well developed, especially with modern recording equipment (including videotapes) and sophisticated sampling techniques. Less developed, however, are the analytical techniques for case studies —

techniques that will provide replicable results from small samples. Nevertheless, the kinds of insights that can be obtained from case studies are so critical to theory construction that the lack of rigor can be tolerated. The need is high—we know of no such studies that are underway—and the speed to completion depends on the number of years encompassed by the design. Since most of the questions we have posed would require long-term studies, speed to completion is assigned a rating of "low."

Case studies have a unique value when they involve interviews in a broad range of schools. The insights obtained by the research staff from firsthand observation within the schools can be invaluable to research design and theory construction. The demands of American graduate student training and professional employment are such that few research psychologists have an opportunity to gain the intimate knowledge of contemporary schools which such interviews would provide.

3. Study of Alternative Curriculum Structures for Secondary Schools

In earlier chapters the need for interchangeability in educational pathways is mentioned repeatedly. Students should be able to select a particular program of study, perhaps only for exploratory purposes, without the strong constraints of continuing in that program until graduation, especially if the program becomes inappropriate to their evolving career plans. It is difficult to structure the high school curriculum offerings to permit such interchangeability and at the same time to preserve sequential integrity in the curriculum. The problem may well have been solved in some high schools, in this country or abroad, or possibly a new conception of the high school curriculum is required.

These questions require the identification of a range of curriculum structures and a detailed examination of the effects of different structures and administrative practices on the career development of the students enrolled. Existing data files such as those of Project TALENT (Flanagan et al., 1962) and *The Base Year Survey of the National Longitudinal Study of the High School Class of 1972* (Hilton and Rhett, 1973) might prove to be useful, although it is likely that such data would have to be extensively supplemented, probably through on-site data collection. The case studies proposed in Item 2 could also provide valuable data.

In addition, it would be desirable to examine the comparative education literature for evidence of the effects of the drastically different curriculum structures existing in other countries. Such a study could make a highly important contribution to secondary school theory and practice in the United States.

A study of alternative curriculum structures would also contribute to the solution of the criterion problem in career development. This difficult problem would be met head-on in designing objective procedures for evaluating the effects of alternative curriculum structures.

COMMENTS

Conducting the study would test the limits of existing technology, primarily because of the criterion problem. How could a researcher demonstrate that the long-term effect of one structure is more beneficial than another? Short-term outcomes, such as greater interchangeability, could be examined, but even high interchangeability may be a mixed blessing.

Nevertheless, it is necessary now to challenge traditional curriculum structures, even though such research may not be highly critical to the implementation of the proposed guidance system. The cost of such a study and the time it would take are difficult to estimate since these factors depend to such a great extent on the design of the study.

4. Evaluation of Alternative Guidance Procedures

In Chapter 2, it was argued that lower cost alternatives to traditional individual student career counseling must be identified and developed. A number of such procedures are known, including self-instructional exercises, classroom procedures, group guidance, simulated occupational exploration, and computerized interactive guidance systems. In evaluating alternative guidance procedures, their relative cost-effectiveness would be assessed by means of literature searches and visits to schools to obtain descriptive information, cost data, and whatever empirical data may be available; and by conventional controlled evaluations of the most promising alternatives. The final product of this step would be a manual for school use describing recommended procedures based on the evaluations conducted.

COMMENTS

It is possible that the necessary judgments could be made by means of expert examination and comparison of evaluations of existing procedures and systems sponsored by USOE and NIE. In this case, the cost would be low and the study could be quickly completed. If existing evaluations are not suitable, then comparison of the competing systems through controlled experiments will be necessary, and the cost would be high, probably in the hundreds of thousands of dollars. But the crucial aspects of such information to the proposed system and to secondary school education in general are important enough to justify the cost.

5. Career Decision-Making Study

The design of any materials and procedures in the general area of career decision making immediately encounters basic questions such as the following:

- Can distinctive styles of decision making be identified and described?
- Are there typologies of decision-making styles? How related are these to other individual or group characteristics (for example, male-female differences)?
- What components of the decision-making process pose the greatest problems for students, and do they differ for subgroups of students?
- Are there systematic differences in decision-making strategies associated with individual differences in cognitive styles?
- What is the effect of educational and cultural background on individual career decision making?[7]

The answers to these questions have important implications for any developmental efforts in the area of decision making. If the kinds of differences implied by the questions do exist, then any materials or procedures designed should be responsive to them in order to maximize their effectiveness. In a very real way, current developmental efforts, however valuable, are proceeding on the basis of assumptions about individual decision making that are largely untested in any rigorous way.

Fortunately, we have an unusual opportunity to investigate

---

7. Again we are struck by the similarity of these questions to those posed independently by Mitchell and her associates (1976).

some, if not all, of these questions through the records that can be
generated for any student who interacts with computer-based guidance and information systems such as SIGI (Katz, 1974). For a selected sample of users, the computer can make a detailed record of
the student's behavior at the terminal. This record includes responses to key displays, the sets of values and specifications the
students use to generate lists of occupations that meet their values
and specifications, the occupations examined, the questions asked,
the predictions called in, the amount of time spent in each component of the system, and so on. Summary data can be accumulated
across all users. Consequently, it is possible to reconstruct a student's behavior from the printout of the tract of a student's path
through the system and to compare it to norms derived from the
summary records. These data, combined with other test data, demographic data, and educational status data about each participant,
make possible numerous, highly relevant analyses at relatively low
cost. The initial analyses would be descriptive and hypothesis-
generating. These would be followed by hypothesis-testing investigations based on independent samples.

COMMENTS

The methodology for the proposed study is adequately developed. Indeed, a first study by Norris (1977) along these lines was
recently completed. Since the data are either available or easily generated, the cost of this research is relatively low, and it can be
completed in a matter of months. Although not highly critical to the
proposed system, more fundamental knowledge about the nature of
human decision making is critical to future developmental work in
career guidance.

6. Survey of Trends in Student Attainments and Characteristics

The concepts and proposals in this book represent a sizable set
of largely untested hypotheses about what influences the outcomes
of secondary school education. Inherent in each step are beneficial
gains in student development. Clearly, however, we can in no way
be certain, on the basis of available evidence, that the outcomes will
be as expected. We cannot accurately predict what may result from
the interaction of the large number of proposed interventions. What
will be the net impact, for example, of increasing expenditures for

instruction in decision making on student attainment in other skills? If gains are made in one area of student development, what price may be paid in other areas? We submit that it is essential to monitor the effects of expenditures along the lines proposed in this book. This is a large order, the nature of which we can only briefly discuss here.

The objective of the study would be to detect changes in the attainments and characteristics of graduating high school seniors in the United States that might result from the introduction of career guidance components such as those discussed in the previous chapters. Attainments and characteristics would be broadly defined to include, for example, traditional academic skills, vocational skills, interpersonal skills, interests, and appreciations. One approach would be to conduct periodic national surveys similar to *The Base-Year Survey of the National Longitudinal Study of the High School Class of 1972* (Hilton and Rhett, 1973). Since the objective of the survey would be substantially less ambitious than the objectives of the original National Longitudinal Study, less instrumentation and a smaller national sample would probably be adequate. The effort would still be large, however. If, for example, the *Base-Year Survey* of NLS were repeated with a sample substantially smaller than the original NLS sample of 21,600, at one-fourth the cost of the original survey, it would still cost roughly $250,000. And to be useful in detecting national trends these surveys, once begun, should be repeated every three or four years.

If the *Base-Year Survey* of NLS were repeated in the spring of 1979, the results, compared with the original survey conducted in the spring of 1972, would provide invaluable data on educational trends for a crucial seven-year period during which numerous schools will have implemented the kind of career guidance components discussed here. The educational trends which could be examined by means of the NLS instruments would include educational and occupational aspirations of high school seniors, attitudes toward schooling, posthigh school plans, reasons for such plans, and basic cognitive skills (as measured by the short battery of tests administered in the NLS *Base-Year Survey*). Such a survey would not, then, provide the kind of comprehensive measurement proposed above, but it would still be valuable and clearly better than no trend data at all.

It could be argued that such periodic national surveys would merely duplicate the National Assessment of Educational Progress

(NAEP). Our preliminary consideration of this alternative suggests, however, that the kind of data being obtained by NAEP will only partially serve the specific purposes outlined. It would be desirable, for example, to be able to relate outcomes to the unique school and work experiences of individual members of the sample, which cannot be done with NAEP data. To enhance its acceptance by the educational community, NAEP was deliberately designed to preclude the relating of test scores to educational treatments.

This matter requires much more study than is possible here. Nevertheless, it is essential that, by one means or another, such monitoring of the impact of innovations in career guidance be conducted.

COMMENTS

Although not critical in the sense that we have used the term concerning the functioning of the comprehensive guidance system, such a study is vital to the well-being of education in the United States. The state of the art of conducting national surveys poses no problems, with the possible exception of the criterion problems we have mentioned repeatedly. Some of the most important educational outcomes, especially in the noncognitive domain, are difficult to measure with the same validity with which we measure cognitive outcomes. How, for example, do we measure a high school senior's motivation to continue lifelong learning? Any progress that a national survey made in the direction of solving this measurement problem would justify the whole effort.

By educational research standards, the cost of periodic national surveys would be substantial; by Pentagon standards, a mere pittance.

7. Career Guidance System and Product Evaluation

There has been less federal support of educational research and development during the last five or six years than in previous years but such research and development has not come to a stop. Educational innovation has continued; new products, teaching materials, and procedures have been developed. To collect and examine the output of the many federal laboratories, state agencies, local school staffs, and private organizations such as ETS and American College Testing Program is a staggering project, and the volume of printed material is well beyond the information-processing capability of any single individual. One wonders how many good ideas and how much good experience lie undiscovered in this avalanche of material.

Beyond the problem of assimilating the huge educational guidance literature is the problem of evaluating the usefulness and promise of the ideas, products, and educational systems that one reads about. Such evaluations were done in the past by USOE's Product Evaluation Panel and two projects sponsored by the National Institute of Education: the Panel Review of Products and the Evaluation of Career Education Materials. Although these projects were well conceived and executed, they cannot fill the continuing need for evaluation. The Educational Products Information Exchange (the EPIE Institute) in New York presumably was designed for this purpose. The consideration of broader federal support of that organization would be a constructive first step.

COMMENTS

Increased effort in this general area would probably require more attention to evaluative procedures and criteria, as Scriven (1967) and others have argued. But all education would profit from such work.

As far as criticalness is concerned, the kind of guidance system discussed in the earlier chapters can be implemented without further evaluation, but, obviously, the possibility of successful innovation is greatly improved by rigorous evaluation of past efforts. Equally important is the ready access to the results of the evaluation.

Assuming that our concern here has been with what might be called secondary evaluation, that is, the weighing, integration, and dissemination of the results of primary evaluations, the cost should not be high, and it should not take long to add substantially to the store of useful evaluative information.

8. Critical Examination of Dropout Literature

The major reason that many students withdraw from secondary school is because they perceive school as irrelevant since they have no career goals, or because they have them and do not understand the relevance of their school experience to them, or because the school experience is, in fact, irrelevant. Although the informal evidence in support of this hypothesis is quite convincing, we do not know of any formal test of the hypothesis — really three hypotheses —

nor do we know of any investigations of the strength of the hypothesis relative to alternative explanations of the withdrawal phenomena. It may be, for example, that the major reason for dropping out is that the quality of school instruction is such that students do not have a sense of personal accomplishment, whether this accomplishment is relevant to their career goals or not. Or the major reason may be the attractiveness of immediate economic gain relative to the value of further gains in skills and knowledge. Or peer group or parental pressures may be dominant. Each of these hypotheses has different implications for educational policy and practice, and each requires investigation.

Also of interest is the other side of the coin: Why do students not drop out? Why do the majority of students stay in school and finish high school (and some continue their education beyond high school)? Is it because the school is perceived by them as being relevant to their careers? Or is it that early acquired values or peer and parental pressures are more powerful than anything the school does? Of particular interest are those students who continue in school even though, on the basis of past research results, we would expect them to drop out.

The primary purpose of this study would not be to discover ways of reducing school withdrawals. For many students, withdrawing from school may be in their best interest. Rather, the purpose of the study would be to study dropouts as a symptom of school malaise. In other words, our interest is in the educational process, and not in dropouts per se. Some dropouts represent education casualties; these dropouts would be of most interest. The objective of the study would be to identify the implications of school withdrawal phenomena for educational planning and guidance practices.

Dropping out has been the subject of innumerable studies. Most, however, have serious shortcomings:

1. They have relied on survey data, the validity of which is subject to serious question.
2. They have relied on retrospective data. In other words, students have been asked after the fact why they dropped out. (There is reason to believe that any retrospective response represents a rationalization that may not reflect the true reason for the act.)
3. They have not taken into consideration the complex multi-

causation of most withdrawals. (There is seldom a single reason for dropping out.)

4. Most dropout studies, not all, have regarded dropping out as a permanent termination of the student's formal education. It is well known that a large percentage of dropouts either return to the school which they left or continue their education in other schools, public and proprietary.
5. Most studies have not taken into consideration the possibility that causation may differ for major categories of students, for example, students categorized by sex, ethnicity, family income, and student ability.
6. Some dropout studies, while fully justified and well done, have been conducted for reasons not directly relevant to our present concerns. For example, they may have been conducted to document the need for special vocational schools.

This is an impressionistic characterization of previous dropout research, based on the authors' past examination of dropout studies for other purposes. A two-phase study would, therefore, be desirable. First, the dropout literature would be critically examined. This examination would include the preliminary results of recently funded dropout studies.

If the results of this examination are as sparse as is expected, the second phase would be designed and conducted as a second study. This study could dovetail nicely with Item 2 (Case Studies) if the dropouts studied were selected from the same schools used for the case studies.

A model for the proposed study of dropout phenomena would be the classic study of juvenile delinquency by the Gluecks (1950), in which the family was identified as the primary factor in a boy's becoming or not becoming a delinquent.

COMMENTS

As with the previous item, this research would contribute to the implementation of any career guidance system but is not critical to the implementation. The cost of evaluating the dropout literature would not be high, but the cost of a large longitudinal study of dropouts would not only equal the several millions invested in the National Longitudinal Study but also would require a number of years to complete. The need for a study of dropouts as a way of studying the educational process is nonetheless high.

9. Study of Current Policy-Planning Activities

To obtain perspective on the impact of federal and state policies related to career guidance, it is important that a baseline be established in the area of policy planning, focusing on the following types of questions:

- What are the current problems that career guidance is addressing?
- What legislation is currently in force, and what is its impact on career guidance programs?
- What are the current local, state, and federal policies regarding career guidance programs?
- How effective are the current legislation and policies in career guidance?
- What current information bases are available to assess the impact of career guidance?
- What is the availability of indicators to assess the impact of career guidance, and what new ones need to be considered?
- What are the alternative approaches to delivering career guidance, and what is their likely impact?

Studies dealing with these and similar types of questions are an ambitious undertaking; however, the consequences of not exploring these questions at this point may seriously deter meaningful evaluation of the impact of career guidance on our nation's students.

COMMENTS

The questions have received some attention from various associations, but in view of the rapidly changing national scene there is a need for up-to-date and continuing examination of policy-planning activities. Thus, although the study is not critical to the implementation of career guidance systems, the need is sufficient to justify the relatively small investment required.

10. Evaluation of Methods of Transmitting Occupational Information

The task is to identify, examine, and design an evaluation of alternative procedures, including instructional materials, to facilitate the acquisition by students of knowledge of occupations. Some procedures that might be included would be planned part-time work, summer work, classroom simulation, automated self-instructional devices, and formal classroom instruction.

Our assumption is that the problem of providing students with opportunities for occupational learning has received sufficient attention nationwide to make the top priority task one of identifying and evaluating the most promising mean or means now available.

COMMENTS

Information about the most effective ways of transmitting information about occupations is sorely needed and is necessary in the implementation of any career guidance system. Since the acquisition of knowledge (not motivation) is in question, the criterion problem encountered by other career research should not be a barrier. However, carefully controlled comparisons of different instructional treatments would be required, and studies of this type are not inexpensive. We would rate the cost and the speed to completion as moderate.

11. Evaluation of Information Files on Occupations

The need is for continuously updated, accurate, and concise descriptions of occupations, structured in such a way that students can learn about broad categories of occupations and also obtain detailed information about specific occupations. Students should have immediate access to information and should be able to obtain copies of information that they regard as personally relevant. Since a large variety of such files exist, the step required is to identify, through a survey of the literature and field trips, the most promising techniques and facilities and to conduct cost effectiveness studies of these facilities.

The objective of this step would be to identify a set of procedures and materials that could be recommended to interested secondary schools.

COMMENTS

Assuming that an elaborate large-scale summative evaluation would not be necessary, the estimated cost of this evaluation work would be low and would not require a long time for completion. Additional expenditures later would be desirable to keep such evaluations complete and up-to-date. Researchers involved in this type of study should become thoroughly familiar with the many relevant projects supported in the past and at present by the United States Department of Labor.

Although the need for additional development of files of occupational information is low—given the extensive work currently underway—the need for a comprehensive inventory and evaluation of alternative methods is high.

12. Comprehensive Criterion Research and Development

Any evaluation of the outcomes of a comprehensive career guidance system obviously requires measurable criteria. Such measures would include scores and other descriptive statistics derived from standardized tests, but would by no means be limited to such scores. Other criteria, derived from the goals of a particular career guidance program, might include job satisfaction, employment, quality of "real-life" decision making, and knowledge of factors entering into training and employment opportunities. Indices such as the proportion of students who are involved in volunteer community activities and the amount and extent of school vandalism might also be useful. One way or another, schools need to be able to measure their progress in achieving whatever goals they set for themselves.

Truly comprehensive criteria need to cover a broad range of outcomes that encompass not only student attainments but also whatever effects the school may have on the student's family and the community.

Since objective tests of student attainment are receiving attention already (see, for example, the College Board's Career Skills Assessment Program), the focus of this study would be on nontest criteria, although the conceptualization of the domain of criteria — the major task—would have to include those outcomes that are measured by conventional tests.

Completing this research and development effort will also require that criterion measures be validated. Some measures, such as the indices mentioned above, will reflect the program objectives so directly that they can be accepted as valid. Other measures, such as self-reported satisfactions, will require empirical demonstration that they are, in fact, measuring what they purport to measure.

COMMENTS

Throughout the country much effort has been directed to identifying the goals and behavioral objectives of career education. One need only examine the huge output of the Ohio State Center for Vocational Education to be convinced of this. There is a pressing need, however, for feasible measures, both test and nontest, of actual outcomes. Accordingly, we would rate the need for this research as high even though it is not critical to implementing a career guidance system.

Since a complex instrument development and data collection effort is involved, the cost would be substantial, and two or three years might be required to complete the effort.

COMPONENT DEVELOPMENT REQUIRED

We now turn to the instruments, materials, procedures, and services necessary to implement a comprehensive guidance system discussed in earlier chapters. Although we describe them as separate components, the reader should keep in mind that this kind of development cannot proceed in a research vacuum, and furthermore, that few of the components can stand alone, without the structure provided by the comprehensive system. Most of the components have been discussed in earlier chapters, and therefore they will be described in less detail than the research studies.

1. Comprehensive Entry Assessment Inventory

The task is to develop a comprehensive inventory of entry assessment measures including, for example, measures of abilities, cognitive style, interests, values, and career awareness, and a brief questionnaire concerning status of career planning and strategies for developing plans. The emphasis of these measures would be on diagnosis as opposed to evaluation, and the measures need not be limited to conventional paper-and-pencil type.

Insofar as possible the measures should be self-administering and self-scoring. But some device, perhaps matrix sampling, would be desirable to permit schools to use some of the results as a baseline for school self-evaluations.

Obviously it will not be necessary to start from scratch. A large number of ability and interest measures are available and also measures of career maturity (see, for example, Super, 1974; the American College Testing Program, 1973–74; and Psychological Corporation, 1975). The problem is to assemble an array of measures that (1) can be administered inexpensively and within a short time (hours, not days), (2) will meet current standards of test validity (See APA, 1974), (3) can provide both individual diagnostic information and data for schoolwide assessment and planning, and (4) can be adapted to a broad range of student ability levels and needs. To give a test which requires at least an eighth-grade reading ability to a student with only fourth-grade ability is pointless. Similarly, high-ability students will be offended by measures that they regard as elementary. Meeting all these requirements will severely strain existing measurement technology. Branching tests and computerized testing techniques may be necessary (Linn, 1969; Lord, 1971; Weiss, 1974).

A preliminary step would be to establish the clear need for each measure and to determine how the results would be used.

COMMENTS

The state of the art for cognitive measures is high — that is, the technology for developing them is highly advanced — but for non-cognitive measures, which are most needed, the state of the art is, at best, moderate. Also, the requirements that an inventory be comprehensive, meet high testing standards, and *also* be inexpensive and require minimal administration time may simply be unfulfillable. At best, some compromise will be necessary. The cost also may be high — in the hundreds of thousands, depending on how many tests have to be developed from scratch. Nevertheless, comprehensive diagnostic assessment on entrance to secondary school is critical to the proposed guidance system, and the available measures are only partially adequate.

2.   Student Self-Survey Instrument

In this step, which is closely related to both the preceding and the following components, the task is to develop classroom-administered, self-scoring materials and procedures for confronting students with the need for early initiation of career planning. A possible approach would be to ask the students, in the form of a self-administered "interview," to record their expectations about high school and their preliminary thinking about their careers. (If the student has done no thinking — which is likely for a large proportion — simply being asked about his or her plans may stimulate such thinking.)

The Self-Survey differs conceptually from Component 1 (Entry

Assessment Inventory) in that the record would be confidential —
possibly highly so — including personal reflections that the students
might not wish to share with anyone, neither teachers, counselors,
nor parents.

Materials to support the Student Self-Survey may include a
teachers' manual, film strips, videotapes, and group guidance materials.

COMMENTS

The state of the art of questionnaire development is high, but
how one would achieve acceptance of this self-survey by the school
staff and how one would motivate students to make full use of this
product, and those that will be recommended next, is an unsolved
problem. It is, however, a critical element in the proposed system.
Whether the need for new material is high or low depends on the
adequacy of materials available, such as those developed for Operations Guidance by the Ohio State University's Center for Vocational
Education (Center for Vocational Education, 1974). In the absence of
a thorough evaluation of these materials, we assign a rating of moderate as far as need is concerned.

The cost and completion time depend, of course, on how much
developmental work is necessary. In any case, developing the self-
survey instrument should be relatively inexpensive and should require less than a year in time.

3. Student Program Planning Procedures

Rational planning by the students is a critical aspect of the proposed system. The need is to develop procedures, including illus-
trative informational materials, for selecting school courses and
work-related experiences on the basis of academic and vocational
knowledge and skills, self-insight, and career knowledge likely to be
gained — procedures which will require minimal face-to-face interaction with guidance counselors.

This product is so closely related to Component 2 and Component 4 that it should be developed in conjunction with them. It is
described separately only because it could conceivably be developed
and used without them, although not with full effectiveness.

A critical aspect of this component is the research that each
school would have to do in order to provide students with information about the probable outcomes of certain choices and, also, with

information about their expected performance in particular educational pathways, based on analysis of past student records. Consider, for example, the school described in Chapter 1, in which 95 percent of the students choosing algebra I subsequently graduated from the college preparatory program in contrast to only 30 percent of the students who chose business arithmetic. The eighth graders in this school system would have profited from knowing this, if for no other reason than to permit them to circumvent the usual pathways if they wished to do so.

A model for a prediction system exists in Palo Alto, California (Palo Alto Unified School District, undated), where procedures and materials for predicting certain student outcomes at the secondary school level were designed and implemented approximately ten years ago. A logical first step in student program planning procedures would be to become thoroughly familiar with the current status of the Palo Alto system and the staff's perception of the most pressing current and future needs.

COMMENTS

Systematic student planning procedures are highly critical to the proposed system. Some schools—like Palo Alto—now provide students with extensive information about the curriculum, but the kind of procedure that we describe here, we believe, is rare. Thus, the need is high. The cost and completion time of this component should not be high.

4.   Student Career Development Log

For this item, the objective would be to develop systematic procedures, including materials for record keeping by students and for periodic review by students of their progress in gaining self-awareness and career planning knowledge and skills. Relevant nonschool experiences would be included in the monitoring by the student.

Again, this product could, and should, be developed in conjunction with others, particularly Component 2 (Student Self-Survey), the discussion of which is relevant to the log.

COMMENTS

The design of the log is straightforward, but the design of procedures and incentives to motivate students to maintain a log would be a challenging task. Materials and procedures developed by Anna

Miller-Tiedeman (1974) appear to be relevant. The need for new procedures depends on the adequacy of procedures such as these. In any case, the procedures are critical, and the cost and completion time should be relatively low.

5. Career Progress Feedback Procedures

This component requires the design and development of procedures by which students can receive feedback on the progress they are making in the formulation of career plans or planning strategies. Traditionally, such feedback has been provided by means of periodic meetings of individual students with guidance counselors. Few schools in the United States, however, have had sufficient staff to provide such service to students, and fewer still are likely to have sufficient staff to provide the expanded services proposed here. What we have in mind, then, is a way of providing students with feedback — a way that makes minimal demands on the time of school personnel.

The task is to design low-cost feedback procedures that do not require electronic data-processing facilities. How this can be done is not clear, but the need is great enough to justify examination of a range of possibilities, including the use of paraprofessionals, student aides, and volunteers.

COMMENTS

Feedback from the environment is a critical aspect of all learning and development, and career development is no exception. The need for developmental work is high; we know of no schools that have solved this problem, with the possible exception of those fortunate enough to have a very low student-counselor ratio. Without a definite plan for the development of this component, we cannot estimate the cost.

6. Model Cumulative Student Data File

The task is to develop a data-processing system, procedures, and facilities for accumulation of student data relevant to all aspects of student development. The difficult issue of who would have access to the files and under what circumstances will have to be resolved. As opposed to the Student Career Development Log (Component 4), which would be maintained by the student and be open to the school staff only at the option of the student, the Cumulative Student Data File should be accessible to the staff and, possibly, parents, depending on what data are accumulated. In other words, the Student Log is a personal log, possibly deeply personal, whereas the Student Data File is quasi-public.

We know of no schools in which student data are not accumulated to some degree. Some schools may have developed highly suitable systems. The task may be, then, one of identifying and evaluating components developed in the past or systems now in place in the field.

COMMENTS

The maintenance of flexible and easily accessed student data files is critical to the proposed system. The required technology is fully developed. The cost of developing this component may be the least of all components, since the task may be one of evaluating the relative strengths and weaknesses of existing data storage systems. Many of the schools may have fully adequate files, and therefore the need for developmental work on the component may be less acute than it is for other components.

7. Decision-Making Instructional Materials

To meet the need for formal instruction in career decision making, a two-phase developmental effort is envisioned. In phase I the adequacy of the decision-making instructional materials currently available (from the College Board, for example) would be formally evaluated. We tentatively propose that this be done through structured interviews with high school seniors who have made full use of the decision-making materials and with faculty and staff members. The evaluations of decision-making instruction by Yabroff (1964) and Miller (1973) are highly relevant to this study. For our present purposes, it is assumed that evidence will be obtained for supplementation of the materials by developing additional text material for student use and additional syllabuses for teachers. (Informal discussions with a number of individuals with firsthand knowledge of decision-making instruction suggest that this is a viable assumption.) Accordingly, the objective of phase II of this step would be to develop and pretest a set of materials and procedures for instruction in career decision making. In so doing, a number of difficult questions will have to be answered:

1. Is career decision making best taught by first teaching general decision-making strategies and then focusing on career decisions, or by some other approach?
2. To what extent can decision making be learned through self-instruction?
3. How do you teach decision making to maximize transfer of skills from the instructional setting to the real-life setting?
4. To what extent, if at all, can career decision-making instruction be divorced from efforts to facilitate the social and personal development of students? The recent work of Miller-Tiedeman and Tiedeman (1975) would indicate that the answer is "not at all."

SIGI shows unusual promise as a means of teaching decision making. However, as with Component 5, Career Progress Feedback Procedures, let us assume that there is an interim—and, probably, continuing—need for written materials to support decision-making instruction.

COMMENTS

Guidance systems such as the one proposed in this book could function without instruction in decision making, although numerous studies of student career planning suggest that the quality of decision making could be much improved (Katz, 1963; Hilton et al., 1962). Also, existing instructional materials may be adequate. Furthermore, until we gain more fundamental knowledge of student decision making, it is not clear what direction developmental work should take. Thus, on several grounds we would assign somewhat lower ratings to this line of work than to other research and development work discussed here.

8. Financial Planning Services

First, selected schools should be surveyed to determine if students are now receiving all the planning help they need (or all the help which it is feasible to provide). If need for further effort is confirmed, the task would be to design and implement a set of procedures and materials to assist students in identifying sources of financial aid for higher education or vocational-technical training and in planning educational expenditures and income-producing activities in the most efficient way.

Despite the importance of students' having access to good financial information and assistance in using it, we will assign a lower priority to developmental work in this area on the basis that it may needlessly duplicate such efforts as the College Scholarship Service (College Board, 1977) and the Early Financial Aid Planning Service (College Board, 1977).

9. Comprehensive Exit Assessment Inventory

The task is to design and implement a comprehensive inventory of measures paralleling at least a fraction of those of the Entry Assessment Inventory (for the purpose of growth scores). The authors' tentative recommendation is that the inventory be administered, typically, early in the senior year, as an aid to postsecondary school planning by the students, although testing in the spring of the senior year may better serve the assessment needs of the school for program planning purposes.

The development of the comprehensive inventory will require precise specification and conceptual analysis of the outcomes to be measured.

Since this item is receiving attention currently and is discussed at some length in earlier chapters, we will not offer additional remarks here. The item is, nonetheless, of major importance.

COMMENTS

For the purpose of establishing priorities, we have assumed that the proposed testing would require two full days (if all tests are given at one time, which may not be desirable), that many of the required measures now exist in usable form, but that as many as ten 40-minute tests will have to be developed from scratch. (An individual student would probably take a small subset of the total inventory of available attainment measures.) Thus, the developmental cost of this item would be substantial.

As with the entry assessment inventory, United States test producers are skilled in the development of cognitive tests but less so in the development of noncognitive measures. Thus the state of the art has to be rated moderate. But such senior year stock-taking is critical to career guidance, from the point of view of both the student and the school, and the need is high.

10.   *Procedures and Materials to Facilitate*
      Senior-Year Career Decision Making

The authors' assumption is that what now passes for senior-year decision making is for some fraction of the students — possibly a large fraction — merely the avoidance or self-defeating postponement of decision making. The student simply goes on to advanced education or accepts a job which happens to be available, without conviction or commitment and without investigating a range of options and making a deliberate rational choice among them. The need, then, is for the design of procedures, equipment, and materials to stimulate and facilitate the processes of making a rational choice.

The choice in question does not necessarily concern a long-term career. For most students, such a choice would be premature. Rather, it concerns the student's next step, either by implementing a tentative career choice or by providing him or her with further experience on which to base a choice.

The effort should also include a survey of available materials, such as American Institutes for Research's *Planning Career Goals* (1976), to minimize the chance of unnecessary duplication.

COMMENTS

How critical this developmental activity is depends on the success of components planned for earlier periods of the secondary school experience. Ideally, by the senior year, students should be skilled and experienced in career planning. It seems unlikely, however, that this ideal will be achieved in the near future and, thus, unlikely that this component will be fairly critical.

Earlier remarks about the state of the art of guidance procedures are relevant here. Cost-effective procedures are desired, and a number of possibilities are receiving attention (for example, group guidance and computer-assisted guidance). But whether one or another will fill the bill remains to be seen. Consequently, on most factors we would assign ratings of moderate to this component.

11.   *Procedures and Materials to Facilitate*
      Job and School Placement

Although vocational-technical high schools and departments seem to be successful in aiding graduates in finding employment, the authors' impression is that the typical comprehensive high school needs innovative procedures and materials to assist all students who desire full- or part-time employment, either before or after graduation. For educational placement, the status may be reversed; that is, comprehensive high schools may do a more effective job than vocational-technical high schools. The effort would require systematic needs assessment, field research, pilot testing of procedures identified or developed, and the preparation of a manual for school use.

This developmental item could easily be combined with the previous item.

COMMENTS

In all respects this item receives ratings of low or moderate: nearly all contemporary schools are concerned with placement, with at least a modicum of success.

12. *Procedures and Instruments for Surveying*
    Exit Career Plans

The instrument would serve several purposes:

1. It would enable school staff to assess the degree to which students have been provided the opportunity and have the incentive to develop their career plans.
2. It would serve as a "posttreatment" measure which, compared with entry survey data, would provide a measure of the impact the school has had on the career development of the students.
3. It would serve as a baseline measure for evaluating the progress students make during the first year after high school and the first five years following high school. For example, were students equipped to implement the plans they had at the time they left high school?

This step would require the design and pretesting of a 5- to 10-page questionnaire that is machine-scorable, with the possible exception of a few open-ended questions. Questionnaires in the public domain, which were developed in a number of large-scale longitudinal studies, may have many usable items.

The currently available *Survey of Plans for Education and Careers* (College Board, 1974) is an excellent start in the direction of satisfying this need. A first additional step would be to conduct a modest survey of schools making use of that instrument. Also, steps might be taken to make sure that results obtained can be compared with data obtained by the National Center for Education Statistics.

Again, this component could be combined with Components 10 and 11.

COMMENTS

This is a lower priority item since it is not essential to the implementation of a guidance system, and some developmental work has already been done in this area. However, it would not be an expensive component and the data obtained would greatly aid a school in monitoring its progress in providing career guidance services.

13. Procedures and Instruments for One-Year and Five-Year Follow-up Surveys

All the comments about Component 12 are relevant here. In addition, a manual would be written providing schools with advice on sampling (where needed), steps to maximize response rates and quality of responses, and—when appropriate—methods of estimating statistical significance of observed changes (e.g., from the first-year follow-up to the fifth-year follow-up).

COMMENTS

Like the previous component, this one is of lower priority. The cost of developing the questionnaires would not be high since extensive use could (and should) be made of items designed for the follow-ups of the *National Longitudinal Study* (Tabler, 1976). If the cost of conducting annual surveys is too great a burden on a school, the surveys could be conducted every three or four years; in large high schools a carefully stratified random sample would be adequate.

If the instruments were designed with an eye to the program-planning needs of state agencies, subsidization of local follow-ups would be a possibility.

14. Secondary School Computer Interactive Guidance System

If SIGI did not exist, the authors would recommend that its development be given the highest priority as the most promising alternative to individual student counseling that we can imagine. Within one system, SIGI satisfies at least six of the requirements we have discussed:

1. A way of confronting students with the status of their career planning.
2. A way of obtaining a record of at least part of the student's thinking about careers.
3. A way of providing students with relevant occupational information.
4. A way of facilitating senior-year decision making.
5. A way of surveying the exit status of the students' career plans.
6. A way of teaching decision-making skills (probably most important).

The format of SIGI is designed for junior college students, but we strongly recommend that the text of SIGI be revised to be suitable for secondary school students. Discussions with Martin Katz, the primary creator of SIGI, indicate that extensive revisions would not be necessary.

As the first step we recommend a thorough investigation of the feasibility of developing a secondary school version of SIGI and making it available to high schools. Such a study would include a consideration of the cost-effectiveness of the alternatives to SIGI, including DISCOVER, the computerized guidance system developed by JoAnn Harris-Bowlsbey (Rayman and Harris-Bowlsbey, 1977); ECES, the system developed under the leadership of Donald Super (Myers, Thompson, Lindeman, Super, Patrick and Friel, 1972); and, also, group guidance procedures.

COMMENTS

The one problem with SIGI for secondary schools is its high initial cost — in the tens of thousands if a junior college has to purchase all the electronic hardware that the system requires. If SIGI were installed in large numbers of high schools, the cost of each installation would be substantially lower. In addition, it is likely that the cost of the necessary hardware will continue to decline as advancements are made in miniaturizing the parts of the system. In any case, the cost of the proposed feasibility study would not be excessive and could generate results with extremely important implications for secondary school career guidance.

How critical this component is depends on the success of efforts to develop noncomputerized methods of satisfying certain systems requirements discussed in the previous chapters. If these efforts fail or are only partly successful—which, we suspect, is likely—a fully developed interactive guidance system like SIGI would be indispensable and, thus, of high criticalness.

15. Simulated Occupational Choice (soc), Phase II

The need for more adequate measures of decision-making skills is unanimously agreed upon. Yet it appears that the approaches to such measurement that have been considered by the ETS and College Board staff are not particularly promising, with the exception of the measures that could result from a continuation of the "Simulated Occupational Choice" study by Katz, Norris, and Pears (1978). This work to date has resulted in the design of a sequence of tasks that simulate the sequence of steps in career decision making. One by-product of the exercise is a set of scales reflecting the student's attainment along several critical dimensions of decision making. Thus, it is now possible to obtain measures with impressive content validity from this individually administered exercise. Additional studies can be undertaken to supplement evidence now being gathered on its construct validity. Then it would be clearly desirable to develop either group-administered or self-administered measures that will produce scores closely related to those obtained on soc, which can serve as a criterion. Whether this is possible remains to be seen.

For the purposes of this chapter we will consider an 18-month developmental effort which would include pilot testing and pretesting of a prototype group-administered instrument to be developed concurrently with research designed to examine further the construct validity of soc.

COMMENTS

Although not critical to the implementation of a career guidance system, a measure of decision-making skill is highly desirable. Whether it is technically possible to develop a group-administered or self-administered version of soc is not certain. But there is a clear need for such a measure for both diagnostic and evaluation purposes.

16.   Materials and Procedures for In-Service Training

In earlier chapters we have argued that providing the full range of needed guidance services will require extensive involvement of classroom teachers, working in collaboration with the guidance staff and the administrative staff. We do not know precisely what is the effective form for this collaboration or what materials are needed. It is certain, however, that teachers, counselors, and administrators will need to learn new ways of interacting with each other, new ways of perceiving students, and new ways of meeting their career guidance needs. To facilitate this learning it is likely that in-service training will be required. (In our interviews with school administrators, the most frequently mentioned need in the area of career guidance was in-service training.) We therefore recommend two steps:

1.   Visits to schools which are known to provide at least some of the career guidance services discussed in this book and which also provide in-service training. The purpose of these visits would be to identify alternative patterns and methods of providing training and the materials needed; to identify the current and future roles of teachers, counselors, and administrators in providing career guidance services; and to identify data bases that have potential use in comprehensive career guidance programs, such as manpower projections, employment trends, sources of financial aid, etc.

2.   Design instructional programs. Some units would be relevant only to teachers or to counselors or to administrators, although we feel strongly that most of the instruction should involve all three groups simultaneously. Since a goal of the instruction would be to achieve change in the way teachers, counselors, and administrators perceive and interact with each other, the program should take advantage of the most advanced techniques in group dynamics.

The instructional staff might initially include staff members of schools which currently have comprehensive career guidance systems. This staff would be augmented by professional staff expertise in career guidance, planning, evaluation, policy analysis, and group dynamics.

COMMENTS

Although not critical as a functioning part of a comprehensive career guidance system, in-service training may be critical as a way of achieving acceptance of the kind of expanded career guidance services discussed here. The need for such training seems to be high, and the cost and completion time are not excessive.

17. Secondary School Guidance Information-
Processing System

One final component discussed in Chapter 4 will need development, namely, an information-processing system to facilitate the efficient flow of information both to and from the following parties: students, the school staff, state agencies, and, in some cases, district and county offices. The system would include means of aggregating data, storing them for both immediate and long-term purposes, and insuring the confidentiality of the data where required. Component 6 (Model Cumulative Student Data File) would be one part of the comprehensive system proposed here.

The outcome of this developmental work would be a systems design, and whatever software and instructional manuals are necessary to enable a local system and state agency, working in collaboration, to implement the system. Extensive field work, systems design, and pilot testing would be required.

COMMENTS

If local systems are to provide information on the career needs of their students to district and state agencies and receive information useful for planning from these agencies, then an efficient information-processing system is critical. The cost would depend on how elaborate the system is, but it should not be high if we assume that extensive software development is not required. The technology necessary is fully developed, and the work should be completed in a matter of months (although the authors' experience is that system design work tends to take longer than anticipated).

SOME RECOMMENDATIONS

Making decisions about what our national priorities should be in the area of career guidance is a complex process involving a broad range of considerations and interested parties. Nevertheless, some tentative recommendations by the authors may help to focus this decision making.

With the exception of cost, the factors were defined to be unidirectional. Other factors being equal, it would seem logical to give priority to an item with a high rating for a given factor. This suggests, in addition, that a simple sum of the ratings (with cost reversed) might serve as the basis for assigning priorities. We question, however, whether a simple sum of the ratings provides a meaningful basis for priorities. Having computed sums — out of curiosity — we are even more sure of the folly of simple sums, particularly in the case of component development. The resulting sums simply do not reflect the importance of certain studies or projects and their functional relationships, primarily because the ratings assigned to certain factors tend to dominate the summary scores. If nothing else, the scores should be standardized and weighted in accordance with their importance. Better still is a more thoughtful, stepwise approach to the necessary decision making, wherein the factors are regarded as pieces of information to be used only when they are relevant.

Research Priorities

We suggest, first, that priority be given to that research which is critical to the implementation of the proposed system. Examination of the ratings, which are summarized in Table 2, indicates that only two studies were rated high in criticalness: evaluation of alternative guidance procedures, and comprehensive criterion research and development. Since evaluating guidance procedures will require a broad range of criterion measures, many of which simply do not exist in suitable form, the conceptualization and development of the needed measures must receive *top priority* (comprehensive criterion research and development) even though the cost may be high and it may take several years to complete the effort. *Second* priority would be given to evaluation of alternative guidance procedures.

Next, we turn to the studies rated moderate in criticalness and rank them in order of their need: *third*, evaluation of methods of transmitting occupational information; *fourth*, longitudinal case studies; and *fifth*, evaluation of alternative curriculum structures for secondary school.

Three studies have ratings of moderate criticalness and moderate need and the same ratings on the other factors. On the basis of

Table 2. SUMMARY OF RATINGS AND PRIORITY RANKINGS FOR RESEARCH STUDIES

Research Study	State of the Art	Criticalness	Cost	Need	Speed to Completion	Priority Ranking
1. National Longitudinal Surveys of Student Development	H	M	L	M	H	8
2. Longitudinal Case Studies	M	M	M	H	L	4
3. Study of Alternative Curriculum Structures for Secondary Schools	M	M	M	H	L	5
4. Evaluation of Alternative Guidance Procedures	H	H	H	H	M	2
5. Career Decision-Making Study	H	L	L	M	H	10
6. Survey of Trends in Student Attainments and Characteristics	H	L	H	H	M	9
7. Career Guidance System and Product Evaluation	H	M	L	M	H	6
8. Critical Examination of Dropout Literature	H	L	L	M	H	11
9. Study of Current Policy-Planning Activities	H	L	L	M	H	12
10. Evaluation of Methods of Transmitting Occupational Information	H	M	M	H	M	3
11. Evaluation of Information Files on Occupations	H	M	L	M	H	7
12. Comprehensive Criterion Research and Development	H	H	H	H	M	1

Table 3. SUMMARY OF RATINGS FOR COMPONENT DEVELOPMENT

			Factors		
Components	State of the Art	Criticalness	Cost	Need	Speed to Completion
1. Comprehensive Entry Assessment Inventory	M	H	H	M	M
2. Student Self-Survey Instrument	M	H	L	M	H
3. Student Program Planning Procedures	H	H	L	H	H
4. Student Career Development Log	M	H	M	M	M
5. Career Progress Feedback Procedures	L	H	?	H	M
6. Model Cumulative Student Data File	H	H	L	M	M
7. Decision-Making Instructional Materials	M	M	?	M	?
8. Financial Planning Services	H	M	L	L	N/A
9. Comprehensive Exit Assessment Inventory	M	H	H	H	M
10. Procedures and Materials to Facilitate Senior-Year Career Decision Making	M	M	M	M	M
11. Procedures and Materials to Facilitate Job and School Placement	H	M	L	L	L
12. Procedures and Instruments for Surveying Exit Career Plans	H	M	L	L	H
13. Procedures and Instruments for One-Year and Five-Year Follow-up Surveys	H	L	L	M	H
14. Secondary School Computer Interactive Guidance System	H	M	M	M	M

| | Factors | | | | |
Components	State of the Art	Criticalness	Cost	Need	Speed to Completion
15. Simulated Occupational Choice (SOC), Phase II	M	M	M	H	M
16. Materials and Procedures for In-Service Training	H	M	M	M	M
17. Secondary School Guidance Information-Processing System	H	H	M	M	M

small differences in criticalness, we would rank these as follows: *sixth*, career guidance system and product evaluation; *seventh*, evaluation of information files on occupations; and *eighth*, national longitudinal surveys of student development.

Of the remaining studies, all of which were rated low in criticalness, one was rated high in need: the survey of trends in student attainment and characteristics. We would rank this study *ninth* even though it would be costly. The remainder of the studies, which have identical ratings, are ranked as follows: *tenth*, career decision-making study (because of the importance of decision making in career development); *eleventh*, critical examination of dropout literature; and *twelfth*, the study of current policy-planning activities.

We are comfortable with these rankings with the possible exception of the relatively low rank (ninth) of item 6 in Table 2 (survey of trends in student attainments and characteristics). We would hope that the pressure of more applied research will not result in the long postponement of such a study.

We also hope that the priority given to criterion development will not detract from the crucial importance of searching out cost-effective alternatives to one-to-one career counseling. In the next section we assign high priority to the development of materials to facilitate planning by students, record keeping by students, and decision making by students. Although we are convinced that students must become the primary agents of their personal development, we cannot imagine how products like the Career Development Log can stand alone, that is, without some kind of facilitating intervention by the school staff. If one-to-one career counseling is not feasible, as we believe, then alternative procedures must be identified.

In addition, we hope that nationwide the research in career guidance will be balanced, including both basic studies (for example, the Career Decision-Making Study) and applied studies.

Product Priorities

To rank the developmental projects, we grouped the items according to their ratings in Criticalness and Need (see Table 3), and then within each group by their combined score on State of the Art, Cost, and Speed. In the case of ties, we ranked the items on the basis of fine differences in criticalness. The final rankings are shown in Table 4.

These decision rules yielded some surprises. The Exit Assess-

Table 4. RANKING OF DEVELOPMENTAL PROJECTS

High Criticalness, High Need
- (3) Student Program Planning Procedures
- (9) Comprehensive Exit Assessment Inventory
- (5) Career Progress Feedback Procedures

Moderate Criticalness, High Need or High Criticalness, Moderate Need
- (2) Student Self-Survey Instrument
- (6) Model Cumulative Student Data File
- (17) Secondary School Guidance Information-Processing System
- (4) Student Career Development Log
- (15) Simulated Occupational Choice (SOC), Phase II
- (1) Comprehensive Entry Assessment Inventory

Moderate Criticalness, Moderate Need
- (14) Secondary School Computer Interactive Guidance System
- (16) Materials and Procedures for In-Service Training
- (7) Decision-Making Instructional Materials
- (10) Procedures and Materials to Facilitate Senior-Year
  Career Decision Making

Moderate Criticalness, Low Need or Low Criticalness, Moderate Need
- (13) Procedures and Instruments for One-Year and Five-Year
  Follow-up Surveys
- (12) Procedures and Instruments for Surveying Exit Career Plans
- (8) Financial Planning Services
- (11) Procedures and Materials to Facilitate Job and School Placement

---

Note: Component numbers are in parentheses.

ment Inventory is second to the Student Program Planner, because of the Inventory's greater cost and questions about the State of the Art of developing the noncognitive measures which are so important to the Inventory. Third in priority are Career Progress Feedback Procedures even though it is not clear whether we have the methodology to develop them.

Developing a secondary school version of SIGI received a relatively low ranking because of the item's ratings of moderate in criticalness and need. If efforts to develop low cost, noncomputerized versions of certain components fail, then the development of a secondary school version of SIGI will become a top priority item. In any case the authors recommend that research and development designed to expand the capability of the existing version of SIGI continue, if only on a modest scale.

In conclusion, we are faced with an unusual opportunity to contribute to career guidance at a highly appropriate time. Career guidance in this country is at a crossroad. It can continue as an ancillary service subject to the vagaries of available funds and administrative whims, or it can become a central factor in the educational process, equal to classroom instruction and administrative functions in facilitating the developing careers of our young people.

CHAPTER 7

Summary and Conclusion

In our conceptualizing of a comprehensive secondary school guidance system, we had two objectives: (1) to help solve the perplexing problems confronting career guidance today, and (2) to provide a framework for research and developmental activities in the area of career guidance. The authors recognized at the outset that facilitating the career development of young people must begin in the early elementary school years and must be articulated with what students do in the years following high school, but the discussion is limited to the secondary school years. We hope that in any subsequent design efforts, by us or others, the years preceding and following secondary school will receive equal attention.

As another way of keeping the task within manageable limits, we restricted the discussion to career guidance even though guidance per se encompasses a broader range of student concerns. We also focused on the role of school personnel in career guidance, thereby slighting the important role of parents, peers, employers, and community leaders. Subsequent work should redress this imbalance.

ASSUMPTIONS

Our conceptualization of secondary school guidance rests on 10 assumptions (Chapter 1) about the desired outcomes of career guidance at the secondary school level and about the nature of school learning, career development, and career decision making.

Assumption 1. When students leave high school, either before or at graduation, they should have carefully planned the next step of their careers and should take this step with as much knowledge as is possible of its probable implications for their developing careers.

Assumption 2. In our rapidly changing world, an individual must have the ability and motivation to adapt to changing environmental demands and opportunities and to keep his or her options open. Career plans properly are perennially tentative, constantly subject to change.

Assumption 3. The career guidance needs of individual students vary over a broad spectrum; what is suitable for one student may well be a needless burden to another.

Assumption 4. It is important for students to gain an understanding of what it means to earn a living and what this requires.

Assumption 5. Academic instruction and work-related experiences gain meaningfulness to students and increased valence when students understand the possible relevance of these experiences to their future work and to productive use of leisure time.

Assumption 6. Career development is a continuous interactive process, inextricably meshed with the total development of the student as a person.

Assumption 7. Decision making relevant to careers continues throughout high school, and in later life as well, and certain early decisions frequently have a critical bearing on subsequent options open to the student.

Assumption 8. The first ingredient of successful career decision making is valid self-knowledge, and this self-knowledge is best obtained through self-analysis of relevant personal experiences.

Assumption 9. The second ingredient of successful career decision making is an accurate knowledge of those occupations that are relevant to each individual student.

Assumption 10.   The primary motivation for student educational development derives from attainment by the student of high standards of excellence.

These assumptions are crucial, although we would be hard put to demonstrate empirically the validity of some of them. It is important to our argument that their validity at least be plausible; otherwise the conceptualization we propose becomes a house of cards.

We do regard the assumptions as plausible, and they do have important implications for career guidance. If, for example, as Assumption 1 states, students should have carefully planned the next step of their careers by the time they leave secondary school, then a huge task is imposed on the schools. Obviously, high school students plan their next steps and always have. The words that make a difference are "carefully," "knowledge," and "implications," for they imply a measure of deliberation, awareness, and rationality which ordinarily is not the rule.

If we also accept Assumption 7, then training in decision making and efforts to increase self-awareness and career awareness must begin early in the secondary school years and, preferably, in elementary school. The task ahead of us becomes a formidable one.

The assumptions also have important implications for allocation of school resources. We are saying, in effect, that our secondary schools must continue to do everything they have done in the past and, in addition, do a better job of satisfying the career needs of students. Yet school resources are limited, and the secondary school calendar is not infinitely expandable. Accordingly, if career development is to be taken seriously by a school system, it should be viewed not as an addition to the present set of experiences in which students engage, but rather as a substantial modification of those experiences, both in academic classrooms and in the many extra-class activities which occupy student and faculty attention. A *re-direction* of present resources and time allocations is called for, as distinct from a new, separate, and added set of learning situations. The intrinsic motivation and self-discipline which career development activities should stimulate could greatly increase the efficiency in the student's use of his or her time and energies.

The place of the counselor in the school takes on larger dimensions under the career development concept. While total student hours in school and total teacher hours in classrooms may remain fairly stable under the "no add-on" assumption, counseling hours, both for individuals and groups, will necessarily increase. This will be particularly true if new and dependable assessment instruments for career counseling are introduced. Accordingly, the only significant "add-on" that is perceived here is the increased involvement of the counseling staff and the teachers in career development activities. With increasing fluidity in school days and hours, the student's access to counselors can be envisioned in time periods quite apart from the conventional school day, including evenings and weekends. The burden of accommodation to the career guidance theme of this book therefore resides in the training of school personnel and the development of materials, procedures, and systems necessary to implement a comprehensive system. This perception of "no add-on" apart from school resources is reflected in the statements of Kenneth Hoyt, Director of Career Education, Office of Education (Hoyt et al., 1972).

COMPONENTS OF A STUDENT GUIDANCE SYSTEM

In spite of the need for more analytical and empirical study of the assumptions, we took them seriously and, in Chapter 2, described the components of a comprehensive guidance system required to achieve the outcomes referred to, directly or indirectly, in our assumptions. These components are as follows:

1. Assessment, at or before high school entrance, of the student's personal characteristics and the status of his or her career planning.
2. Student selection of high school courses on the basis of their relevance to the student's developing plans or strategy for developing plans.
3. At the completion of each academic or vocational course, review by students of the possible career implications of their experience in the course.
4. Valid occupational sampling by the student.
5. Feedback and self-monitoring of career planning progress.
6. Procedures for group guidance and self-guidance.
7. Access to a variety of types of information about the spectrum of occupations.
8. Acquisition of decision-making skill.

9. Interchangeability of educational pathways with minimal penalty to the student.
10. Assistance in financial planning.
11. Comprehensive assessment of attainment in the senior year.
12. Aids and incentives for senior-year commitments.
13. Assistance in job placement.
14. Exit survey of career plans.
15. Posthigh school follow-up of each graduating class.

The key concept inherent in these components is that of early confrontation, planning, testing, and reformulation. This is, of course, not a new concept, except possibly for the emphasis on confrontation. We are saying that early in high school students must be confronted with the need to begin seeking information about career alternatives thoughtfully and deliberately and to begin evaluating their personal strengths, weaknesses, interests, values, and goals.

Although several components of the comprehensive system are designed to make students aware of this need for early confrontation, we still view the means of achieving such confrontation as a problem needing further study. The human tendency to avoid confrontation is strong, particularly when one's own behavior is involved. Moreover, the realities of occupational economics can be unpleasant. But if students are to be fully prepared in secondary school for the next step of their careers, whether this be continued education or immediate employment, the preparation must begin early in secondary school. We see no alternative.

We encountered a dilemma in this area, however. On the one hand, we argued that students should formulate tentative plans in order that these plans might be tested, reformulated, tested again, etc. Thus, students should make educational commitments, however tentative. On the other hand, we argued that students should keep their options open and avoid committing themselves to educational pathways from which it is difficult to transfer. We still view this as a dilemma that places a premium on students' developing effective strategies for career exploration—strategies that will permit them to immerse themselves in a line of study and still be able to switch to another line of study if their first selection proves to be unrewarding.

These strategies will vary from student to student, depending upon the unique abilities, needs, values, and goals of each student and upon his or her financial resources. One strategy cannot be prescribed for all students, which means that a high premium is placed on skillful career counseling and effective support systems and materials.

A premium is also placed on thoughtful curriculum planning by the faculty, guidance staff, and administration, to achieve a curriculum structure that allows both commitment and mobility. Because we view this as a problem requiring further study, we recommend a study of alternative curriculum structures in Chapter 6.

Another dilemma concerns how much of a high school student's time should be expended directly in relation to future careers, in contrast to learning for the sake of learning. The emphasis of the components we describe in Chapter 2 is clearly on efficient, purposeful, considered selection of courses. On the other hand, we believe that high school should be a period of wide-ranging, adventurous exploring, including taking some subjects just for the fun of it. Our resolution of this dilemma is to acknowledge that surely some subjects should be taken for simple enjoyment, but that when this is done the student should perceive the experience as an opportunity to gain self-insight and, perhaps incidentally, knowledge of occupations. In other words, our proposal should in no way be interpreted as requiring that every high school course have direct and immediate vocational relevance.

A CONCEPTUAL MODEL OF THE STUDENT DEVELOPMENT PROCESS

In Chapters 3 and 4 we focused on the total guidance system, first on a conceptual level and then on a less abstract, operational level. We proposed that the student be viewed as a complex information-processing system exposed over time to a barrage of informational inputs from the environment. But unlike conventional computers, students are transformed by the experience, that is, students learn. They also have a kind of control over the environment which makes them different from computers: They can select what inputs they pay attention to and ultimately can transform their environment and make it more conducive to their own development. This is a key concept. Students need not be the passive recipients of information — they can become the active agents of their progress.

To highlight the features of our proposed system, we contrasted it with a hypothetical traditional school. In this traditional school, decisions, such as course selections, are made largely on the basis of the student's past performance and to an unknown but probably large extent by other persons in the student's environment (teachers, counselors, and parents).

We hypothesized that the critical decision on what the student in our *traditional* school does after high school was based on six major informational inputs: emotions and beliefs, self-perceptions, family and peer influences, counselor perceptions, educational and occupational information, and decision making by postsecondary schools and employers. Thus, again, student decision making is influenced to a large extent by other decision makers and factors over which the student has little control.

In the proposed system the process differs in three major ways. First, and most important, students themselves occupy the central role in evaluating their progress, in formulating strategies for developing their career plans, and in deciding which courses and what related experiences they will involve themselves in. Second, students have much more information available to them — about their personal characteristics, their performance, the occupational and educational environment, and the state of the economy. Third, guidance functions are substantially broadened.

We characterized the traditional career counselor primarily — not entirely, of course — as a gatekeeper, record keeper, and purveyor of information, while the proposed counselors were described as student development specialists. In this new role the counselors function as collaborators with the instructional staff in arranging learning experiences, as specialists in the assessment of student characteristics and broad educational outcomes, as specialists in information processing, storage, and retrieval, and as experts in facilitating student decision making.

In the proposed system the student is in the driver's seat, selecting courses on the basis of his or her tentative career plans, or strategies for developing plans, making informed and deliberate decisions, and creating career opportunities rather than passively responding to them. The total system is shown in Figure 6. Such a system may have been the goal of *some* high school guidance staffs for many years. Our impression, however, is that few staffs have succeeded in achieving it.

The proposed system implies new functions, roles, and relationships among administrators, teachers, guidance personnel, students, parents, and members of the community. In an admittedly overdrawn description of the traditional system, we described, in Chapter 4, these roles as compartmentalized, with limited interaction among the participants. The chief contacts of the guidance staff, for example, are with students on a one-to-one basis for one of two specific purposes, either to assist in setting up students' schedules or to assist in postsecondary school placement. Information also tends to be compartmentalized. Staff members maintain separate files to suit their own needs with relatively little sharing of information between teachers and guidance staff. Furthermore, the focus is on information about, not *for*, the students.

In the proposed system, however, we hypothesize much more interaction among the participants in the system and much more sharing of information. The distinctions between teachers and career guidance counselors diminish as each assumes more responsibility for student career development. The guidance staff members function both as catalysts and as coordinators of a social system that involves teachers, students, parents, and employers as active participants. Students become directing agents in their career development rather than directed elements.

The more complex and extensive information requirements of the proposed system are also discussed in Chapter 4. The general objective of the information system is to facilitate the students' learning, inquiry, assessment, and decision-making processes, and to support the schools' responsibilities for operating, monitoring, and evaluating the students' progress. The total system is divided into three subsystems: the student subsystem, the school subsystem, and the state subsystem, with information flowing both to and from each subsystem.

A critical aspect of the student subsystem is the need to protect the student's privacy. To this end we propose that certain personal information be entered into the subsystem by the student and be accessible thereafter only to him or her. Other student information is collected and released as summary data at the school and state levels where the data are necessary for the operation and evaluation of the system. Exactly how this distinction will be implemented remains to be seen, but, in principle, it is a solvable technical problem.

Finally, we provided an illustration of how the student career guidance system might function (at the risk of appearing to be more sure of specific features of the system than we are). In reading this section, one is struck by the similarity between what is proposed and what is in place, in part at least, in many schools today. If there is any originality in our proposal, it is in the way in which we have integrated a large number of components into a comprehensive system.

IMPLEMENTATION

Implementing the total system poses many problems. Trying, in Chapter 5, to confront these problems was a sobering experience.

The major problem is, not unexpectedly, financial. Cost considerations create yet another dilemma. On the one hand, we propose a broadening and intensification of the guidance function; on the other hand, we recognize a pressing need to minimize additional school costs. There are definite signs of change in the schools along the lines that we propose. But much remains to be done, and the cost to most local school systems will be large. Although some federal and state level funds are likely to be available, our assumption is that such funding cannot be expected to cover all the costs of all innovations in all school systems on a continuing basis.

Some other problems discussed in Chapter 5 are:

1. Strong resistance in powerful quarters to testing in the cognitive domain.
2. The limitations or absence of suitable measures in the noncognitive domain.
3. The need to safeguard the confidentiality of student data.
4. The constraints on innovation imposed by requirements mandated by state legislatures.
5. The questionable validity of current opportunities for students to sample occupations.
6. The shortage in the schools of the kind of expertise required by expanded test programs, by new curriculum units in career decision making and occupational information, and by complex information-processing systems.
7. The difficulty of motivating students to recognize the need to engage in early career planning and exploration.
8. Resistance to guidance innovations by other professional groups competing for school resources.
9. Resistance by community interests to any innovation that will increase the size of the school budget.

Faced with these problems, especially the realities of school financing, what steps can we recommend to make possible the implementation of the comprehensive system proposed? The first and most salient recommendation is that implementing the total system should proceed on a stepwise, modular basis. A wide berth should be given to the tendency to prepare huge prepackaged programs. But this approach creates a problem. The system we have proposed is, indeed, a system in the sense that many of its components are interdependent. They cannot stand alone and function with full effectiveness. The functioning of the Student Log, for example, assumes that students will have an opportunity to assess their personal attributes and will receive extensive feedback from the school environment on their career planning progress, and that individual student initiative will be supported by teachers and counselors who have accepted the philosophy of the system and have the skills to make it work. This is a large order. Yet we see no alternative to the stepwise modular approach in most schools. This will place a premium on the most careful planning by the schools. Schools will need extensive assistance in identifying ways of reducing internal expenses and obtaining technical advice.

We recommend further that components of the proposed system be tested in local pilot situations rather than in full-blown state programs and that schools be prepared to start from scratch with local needs assessment and recognize that their needs may be unique. The wheel may have to be reinvented repeatedly.

PRIORITIES FOR RESEARCH DEVELOPMENT

We view the remarks in Chapter 5 concerning the problems of implementation as sound and realistic, however humbling. Obviously there are many unsolved problems. Chapter 6, in which 12 possible research studies and 17 components are proposed, outlines a broad program of research and development with an eye to solving some of these problems. If the need for component development were not so pressing, we would recommend an exclusive focus on the many fundamental research questions that arise in discussing our assumptions and the components required by the comprehensive system. The whole system rests on a fragile foundation of fundamental knowledge. But we concluded that component development cannot wait for answers to all our questions and must proceed on the basis of the best available evidence, while at the same time research efforts continue to add to this evidence. We propose that 20 percent of available funds be allocated for general research in the area of career development and decision making and 80 percent for product and service development. Although we would be hard put to specify precise figures, we feel the 20 percent recommended for research is a minimum.

The research studies are rated by the authors on five factors: State of the Art, Criticalness, Cost, Need, and Speed to Completion. The services and products are rated on the same factors. Using these factors in a stepwise fashion (as opposed to obtaining a simple sum of the ratings), the items are ranked from top priority to lowest priority. In the ranking of the research studies, top priority was given to the development of comprehensive criteria and, then, in view of the crucial importance of identifying cost-effective alternatives to one-to-one counseling, the evaluation of alternative guidance procedures was given second priority. The full list of research studies in order of decreasing priority is as follows:

Comprehensive Criterion Research and Development
Evaluation of Alternative Guidance Procedures
Evaluation of Methods of Transmitting Occupational Information
Longitudinal Case Studies
Evaluation of Alternative Curriculum Structures for Secondary Schools
Career Guidance System and Product Evaluation
Evaluation of Information Files on Occupations
National Longitudinal Surveys of Student Development
Survey of Trends in Student Attainments and Characteristics
Career Decision-Making Study
Critical Examination of Dropout Literature
Study of Current Policy-Planning Activities

Our one uneasiness is with the relatively low rank which was given to the survey of national trends in student attainments and characteristics. The low rank was given primarily because the survey is not critical to implementing the proposed system and its cost would be substantial. The rank does not reflect the crucial importance of the survey. Our deep concern is that innovation in the area of career guidance, however well-intentioned, could have unanticipated and undesired side effects. The American high school represents an equilibrium, possibly unstable, between many opposing forces. If it is an unstable equilibrium, innovation could result in a cascading pileup of negative effects. We think this possibility is remote, but since it does exist we recommend that careful steps be taken to monitor trends in the outcomes of secondary school education. Because this will involve large annual expenditures, we assume that the research will require federal support.

In the component area, highest priority was given to the development of student program planning procedures, because of their high criticalness and high need. The complete list in order of decreasing priority is as follows:

Student Program Planning Procedures
Comprehensive Exit Assessment Inventory
Career Progress Feedback Procedures
Student Self-Survey Instrument
Model Cumulative Student Data File
Secondary School Guidance Information-Processing System
Student Career Development Log
Simulated Occupational Choice (soc), Phase II
Comprehensive Entry Assessment Inventory
Secondary School Computer Interactive Guidance System
Materials and Procedures for In-Service Training
Decision-Making Instructional Materials
Procedures and Materials to Facilitate Senior-Year Career
    Decision-Making
Procedures and Instruments for One-Year and Five-Year Follow-
    up Surveys
Procedures and Instruments for Surveying Exit Career Plans
Financial Planning Services
Procedures and Materials to Facilitate Job and School Placement

We recognize that unresolved issues remain and that what we have proposed needs further consideration, refinement, and possible reformulation. We hope, however, that this book at least defines the issues and will serve as the basis for planning sound programs of research and development in career guidance throughout the country. Educational research and development does, indeed, have an extraordinary opportunity to contribute to career guidance at a highly appropriate time.

Bibliography

American College Testing Program, *Assessment of Career Development.* Iowa City: American College Testing Program, 1973.

American Institutes for Research, *Planning Career Goals.* Monterey, Calif.: CTB/McGraw-Hill, 1976.

American Psychological Association, *Standards for Educational and Psychological Tests.* Washington, D.C.: American Psychological Association, 1974.

Boocock, S. S., and E. O. Schild, eds., *Simulation Games in Learning.* Beverly Hills, Calif.: Sage Publications, 1966.

Borow, H., "The Development of Occupational Motives and Roles," in *Review of Child Development Research,* Vol. 7, L. W. Hoffman and M. L. Hoffman, eds. New York: Russell Sage Foundation, 1966.

Boyd, J. L., and B. Shimberg, *Directory of Achievement Tests for Occupational Education.* Princeton, N.J.: Educational Testing Service, 1971.

Boyd, J. L., and B. Shimberg, *Handbook of Performance Testing: A Practical Guide for Test Makers.* Princeton, N.J.: Educational Testing Service, 1971.

Campbell, R. E., "Application of Systems Approaches to Career Guidance Programs," *Focus on Guidance,* Vol. 4, No. 8, 1972, pp. 1–11.

Campbell, R. E., "Career Guidance Practices Transcending the Present," *Vocational Guidance Quarterly,* Vol. 22, 1974, pp. 292–301.

Campbell, R. E., G. R. Walz, J. V. Miller, and S. F. Kriger, *Career Guidance: A Handbook of Methods.* Columbus, Ohio: Charles E. Merrill, 1973.

Center for Vocational Education, *Operations Guidance, Steering Committee Handbook.* Columbus, Ohio: Ohio State University, 1974.

Circle, D. F., A. Kroll, D. Clemens, and D. Overholt, *The Career Information Service.* Boston: Bureau of Vocational Education, Department of Education, 1968.

Coleman, J. S., *The Adolescent Society: The Social Life of the Teenager and Its Impact on Education.* New York: Free Press, 1967.

College Entrance Examination Board, *The College Scholarship Service.* New York: College Entrance Examination Board, 1977.

College Entrance Examination Board, *Introducing the Early Financial Aid Planning Service.* New York: College Entrance Examination Board, 1977.

College Entrance Examination Board, *Survey of Plans for Education and Careers.* New York: College Entrance Examination Board, 1977.

Crites, J. O., "A Comprehensive Model of Career Development in Early Adulthood," *Journal of Vocational Behavior,* Vol. 9, No. 1, 1976, pp. 105–118.

Crites, J. O., *Vocational Psychology.* New York: McGraw-Hill, 1969.

Dillenbeck, D. D., *A Report to the Trustees of the College Entrance Examination Board: Guidance Services, 1968–1973.* New York: College Entrance Examination Board, September 1968.

Flanagan, J. C., J. T. Dailey, M. F. Shaycoft, W. A. Gorham, D. B. Orr, and I. Goldberg, *Design for a Study of American Youth.* Boston: Houghton Mifflin, 1962.

Ginzberg, B., S. W. Ginsburg, S. Axelrad, and J. L. Herman, *Occupational Choice: An Approach to a General Theory.* New York: Columbia University Press, 1951.

Glueck, S., and E. Glueck, *Unraveling Juvenile Delinquency.* New York: Commonwealth Fund, 1950.

Gribbons, W. D., and P. R. Lohnes, *Emerging Careers.* New York: Teachers College Press, Columbia University, 1968.

Grubb, W. N., and M. Lazerson, "Rally 'Round the Workplace: Continuities and Fallacies in Career Education," *Harvard Educational Review,* Vol. 45, 1975, pp. 451–674.

Gysbers, N. C., H. N. Drier, and E. J. Moore, *Career Guidance.* Worthington, Ohio: Charles A. Jones, 1973.

Hansen, L. S., *Career Guidance Practices in School and Community.* Washington, D.C.: National Vocational Guidance Association, 1970.

Hansen, L. S., and W. W. Tennyson, "A Career Management Model for Counselor Involvement," *Personnel and Guidance Journal,* Vol. 53, 1975, pp. 638–646.

Harris, J., "The Computer: Guidance Tool of the Future," *Journal of Counseling Psychology,* Vol. 21, 1974, pp. 331–339.

Herr, E. L., *Decision-Making and Vocational Development*. Boston: Houghton Mifflin, 1970.

Herr, E. L., and S. H. Cramer, *Vocational Guidance and Career Development in the Schools: Toward a Systems Approach*. Boston: Houghton Mifflin, 1972.

Hilton, T. L., R. Baenninger, and J. H. Korn, *Cognitive Processes in Career Decision-Making*. Final report, Cooperative Research Project No. 1046. Pittsburgh: Carnegie Institute of Technology, 1962.

Hilton, T. L., A. E. Beaton, and C. P. Bowers, *Stability and Instability in Academic Growth — A Compilation of Longitudinal Data*. Final report to USOE, Research No. 0-0140. Princeton, N.J.: Educational Testing Service, 1971.

Hilton, T. L., and H. Rhett, *The Base-Year Survey of the National Longitudinal Study of The High School Class of 1972*. Final report to the U.S. Department of Health, Education, and Welfare, Office of Education, National Center for Education Statistics. Princeton, N.J.: Educational Testing Service, June 1973.

Hoyt, K. B., R. N. Evans, E. F. Mackin, and G. L. Magnum, *Career Education. What It Is and How To Do It*. Salt Lake City: Olympus, 1972.

Jepsen, D. A., and J. S. Dilley, "Vocational Decision-Making Models: A Review and Comparative Analysis," *Review of Educational Research*, Vol. 44, 1974, pp. 331–349.

Jones, G. B., C. B. Helliwell, and L. H. Ganschow, "A Planning Model for Career Guidance," *Vocational Guidance Quarterly*, Vol. 23, 1975, pp. 220–226.

Jordaan, J. P., "Life Stages as Organizing Modes of Career Development," in *Vocational Guidance and Human Development*, E. L. Herr, ed. Boston: Houghton Mifflin, 1974.

Jöreskog, K. G., "A General Method for Analysis of Covariance Structures," *Biometrika*, Vol. 57, 1970, pp. 239–251.

Katz, M. R., *Decisions and Values: A Rationale for Secondary School Guidance*. New York: College Entrance Examination Board, 1963.

Katz, M. R., SIGI, *A Computer-Based System of Interactive Guidance and Information*. Princeton, N.J.: Educational Testing Service, 1974.

Katz, M. R., L. Norris, and L. Pears, "Simulated Occupational Choice: A Diagnostic Measure of Competencies in Career Decision Making," *Measurement and Evaluation in Guidance*, Vol. 10, 1978, pp. 222–232.

Kroll, A. M., Dinklage, L. B., Morley, E. D., Wilson, E. H., and Lee, J. *Career Development: Growth and Crisis*. New York: John Wiley & Sons, 1970.

Krumboltz, J. D., "A Social Learning Theory of Career Decision Making," in *A Social Learning Theory of Career Decision-Making*, A. M. Mitchell,

G. B. Jones, and J. D. Krumboltz, eds. Palo Alto, Calif.: American Institutes for Research, 1975.

Linn, R. L., D. A. Rock, and T. A. Cleary, "The Development and Evaluation of Several Programmed Testing Methods," *Educational and Psychological Measurement,* Vol. 29, 1969, pp. 129–146.

Lord, F. M., "The Self-Scoring Flexilevel Test," *Journal of Educational Measurement,* Vol. 8, 1971, pp. 147–151.

Marland, S. P., Jr., "A Proposal for a Comprehensive System of Testing for Job Entry," in *Report of the Commission on Tests — II, Briefs.* New York: College Entrance Examination Board, 1970.

Marland, S. P., Jr., *Career Education: A Proposal for Reform.* New York: McGraw-Hill, 1974.

Miller, G. P., "The Impact of a Decision-Making Curriculum on Junior and Senior High School Students." Unpublished doctoral dissertation, Teachers College, Columbia University, 1973.

Miller-Tiedeman, A., *Individual Career Exploration* (ICE). Bensenville, Ill.: Scholastic Testing Service, 1974.

Miller-Tiedeman, A., and D. V. Tiedeman, "Choice and Decision Processes and Careers." Paper presented at the Conference on Career Decision Making, American Institutes for Research, Illinois, March 1975.

Mitchell, A. M., and J. A. Saum, *A Master Plan for Pupil Services.* California Personnel and Guidance Association, 1972, No. 4.

Mitchell, A. M., G. B. Jones, and J. D. Krumboltz, eds., *A Social Learning Theory of Career Decision Making.* Palo Alto, Calif.: American Institutes for Research, 1976.

Myers, R. A., A. Thompson, R. Lindeman, D. Super, T. Patrick, and T. Friel, ECES: *Report of a Two-Year Field Trial.* New York: Teachers College Press, Columbia University, 1972.

National Association of Secondary School Principals. *Secondary Schools in a Changing Society: This We Believe.* Reston, Va.: National Association of Secondary School Principals, 1975.

National Panel on High Schools and Adolescent Education Report. Washington, D.C.: U.S. Department of Health, Education, and Welfare, 1974.

Norris, L., "Sex Differences in the Career Decision-Making Process," NIE G-77-002. Proposal submitted by Educational Testing Service, Princeton, N.J., to National Institute of Education.

Osipow, S. O., *Theories of Career Development,* 2nd edition. New York: Appleton-Century-Crofts, 1973.

Palo Alto Unified School District, "Conference Summary — from Theory to Practice: The Description and Demonstration of a Guidance Program in One District K-12." Unpublished and undated.

Peng, S. S., C. E. Stafford, and R. J. Talbert, *National Longitudinal Study of* the High School Class of 1972 — Review and Annotation of Study Reports. Research Triangle Park, N.C.: Research Triangle Institute, 1977.

Prediger, D., "The Role of Assessment in Career Guidance," in Vocational Guidance and Human Development, E. L. Herr, ed. Boston: Houghton Mifflin, 1974.

Psychological Corporation, DAT Career Planning Program. New York: Psychological Corporation, 1975.

Rayman, J., and J. Harris-Bowlsbey, "DISCOVER: A Model for a Systematic Career Guidance Program," Vocational Guidance Quarterly, Vol. 26, 1977, pp. 3–12.

Scriven, M., "The Methodology of Evaluation," in Perspectives of Curriculum Evaluation, AERA Monograph Series on Curriculum Evaluation, No. 1. Chicago: Rand McNally, 1967.

Shertzer, B., and S. C. Stone, Fundamentals of Counseling, 2nd edition. Boston: Houghton Mifflin, 1974.

Skinner, B. F., Science and Human Behavior. New York: Macmillan, 1953.

Sprinthall, N., Guidance for Human Growth. New York: Van Nostrand Reinhold, 1971.

Strong, E. K., Jr., Vocational Interests of Men and Women. Stanford, California: Stanford University Press, 1943.

Super, D. E., "A Theory of Vocational Development," American Psychologist, Vol. 8, 1953, pp. 185–190.

Super, D. E., The Psychology of Careers. An Introduction to Vocational Development. New York: Harper Bros., 1957.

Super, D. E., R. Starishevsky, N. Matlin, and J. P. Jordaan, Career Development: Self-Concept Theory. New York: College Entrance Examination Board, 1963.

Super, D. E., ed., Measuring Vocational Maturity for Counseling and Evaluation. Washington, D.C.: National Vocational Guidance Association, 1974.

Tabler, K. A., National Longitudinal Study of the High School Class of 1972 — Tabular Summary of First Followup Questionnaire Data. Washington, D.C.: U.S. Government Printing Office, 1976.

Tiedeman, D. V., "Structuring Personal Integration into Career Education," Personnel and Guidance Journal, Vol. 53, 1975, pp. 706–711.

Varenhorst, B., "The Life Career Game: Innovative Tool for Group Counseling," The School Counselor, Vol. 15, 1968, pp. 362–375.

Weiss, D. J., Strategies of Adaptive Ability Measurement, Research Report 74-5, Psychometric Methods Program, Department of Psychology, University of Minnesota, 1974. Contract No. N00014-67-A-0113-0029, NR No. 150-343, with the Personnel and Training Research Programs, Psychological Sciences Division, Office of Naval Research.

White, R. W., *Lives in Progress: A Study of the Natural Growth of Personality*. New York: Dryden Press, 1952.

Willingham, W., W., R. I. Ferrin, and E. P. Begle, *Career Guidance in Secondary Education*. New York: College Entrance Examination Board, 1972.

Yabroff, W. W., *An Experiment in Teaching Decision-Making*, Research Report No. 9. Sacramento, California: State Department of Education, 1964.

Index